APPROACHING CHINA

走近中国

上
Shanghai
海

Shen Yicheng

Shanghai People's Fine Arts Publishing House

Contents

Chapter3 Features · Shanghai

Contents

Shanghai is a sea city. It neighbors the sea into which the Yangtze River flows through here. Although younger than those cities with centuries-old history and grand imperial palaces, Shanghai's feature is most apparent in its vigor and livingness.

Shanghai is deep like a sea. It opens its arms wide and welcomes whatever and whoever from the all corners of the world. It is this magnanimity and comprehensibility that make Shanghai a cosmopolitan city.

Shanghai is colorful like a sea. Either the material abundance or the spiritual enrichment helps make Shanghai a fresh and enchanting city.

Shen Yicheng, China

1

No city can live without history. A city without history is as gossamer and superficial as a man without background. As the most flourishing international metropolis in modern China, Shanghai has always been regarded as a city that thrived fleetly during more or less than one hundred years. While the fact is that Shanghai, who occupies an area of 6,341 sq. km., also boasts a brilliant and gorgeous history of long standing, which is part of the splendid culture of the Chinese nation and which is often neglected. During several decades, archeologists have already found in Shanghai about 30 historical sites that can be traced back as early as 4,000 to 6,000 years ago. They respectively reflect the times of the early, middle and late stages of the matrilineal society, the patrilineal clan commune, as well as the period of class society. All these archaeological discoveries help to ascertain that the history of Shanghai can be traced back to 6,000 years ago.

Six-Thousand-Year-Old Majiabang Culture

Paddy-marked Potteries of Majiabang Culture

Majiabang Culture is one of the ancient cultures appeared as early as the matrilineal society in the Taihu Lake valley and ever since 1959 has been named after Majiabang of Jiaxing City of Zhejiang Province, the place where its historical site was excavated. In Shanghai, however, the most representative ones are the lower layers of Songze Historical Site of Qingpu District and the Zhashan Historical Site of Jinshan District. The fact that many varieties of cultivated paddies have been found in these two historical sites, has vividly proved that the ancestors of Shanghai started planting paddies 6,000 years ago. In those days, people produced in the manner of slash-and-burn cultivation by cutting down trees with stone axes and burning them into ashes for fertilizer. Livestock breeding was also of great importance in the economy at that time for quite a few pig bones and tusks were excavated from the historical sites. The simple and rustic handmade potteries like kettle, pot, crock, basin and vessel were the main daily appliance in ancient time.

Within 100 years, Shanghai developed itself from a fishing village into a metropolitan city.

Five-Thousand-Year-Old Songze Culture

In 1960, a group of graves have been found and a passel of typical household utensils have been excavated in the middle layer of the Songze Historical Site in Qingpu District, from where Songze Culture derived its name. Songze Culture is the continuance of Majiabang Culture and the predecessor of Liangzhu Culture. All together there were 97 graves and the No. 84 grave buried the remains of both mother and son, clearly revealing the custom of the matrilineal society that the children only knew their mothers. The craftwork of potteries and techniques of polishing the pottery bases, brims, bodies and feet were improved a lot and made the potteries shapely and smooth. Unique forms, various types and colored drawings have clearly shown the original cultural creativity of the ancestors of Shanghai. For instance, there is a chunky grey pottery with three equidistant thin mouths. But how can we pour water from a pot like this? Therefore, experts believe this is a three-mouth drinking vessel which was used for celebrations in clan societies. People inserted straws and shared the wine inside the pot. Up to the present, people in remote districts still carry on this custom. And it could be presumed that the ancestors of Shanghai had the habit of making and drinking wines.

Shanghai's cradled by water and boats.

Ancient Drinking Vessel   Ancient Cooking Vessel   Three-footed Ancient Utensil

Four-Thousand-Year-Old Liangzhu Culture

Jade Ring-Ancient Ornament

Boasting exquisite jade articles, Liangzhu Culture is named after the place Liangzhu of Yuhang, Zhejiang Province where it was excavated for the first time in 1936. Historical sites of this culture were also discovered in places of Shanghai, such as Maqiao District, Jinshan District, Songjiang District, Qingpu District and Jianghai Village of Fengxian District. In Fuquanshan Historical Site of Qingpu District, in particular, archeologists found many fine and exquisite jade pendants, gems and jade axes, clearly showing the skilled craftwork in those days. All of these jade articles are either funerary objects or sacrificial utensils, and have verified the upgrade of the status of mankind. The agriculture at that time has entered the plough age because big sharp-edged triangle stone ploughs with three holes as well as stone reaphooks were been excavated. Potteries in those days were made resembling wheels and aboriginal symbols and characters appeared on them. Graves of slaves buried alive with their deceased masters were also excavated, showing the great disparity of people caused by the development of social production. All these evidences have revealed that a new society was on the verge of development and the ancestors of Shanghai were expanding towards eastern beachfront.

Now Fuquanshan Historical Site, this massif of 70 meters high that are famous for its luscious well water, is listed as a major historical and cultural site under state protection. It is the headstream of the history of Shanghai.

Characters and Signs on Ancient Potteries

Fishing Port

Small Fishing Net Develops Big Shanghai

Small fishing net and big Shanghai seem to be two totally unrelated items, while it is exactly the small fishing net that brought the grandness of big Shanghai and vividly tells the predecessor of Shanghai.

Shanghai is actually a shoal and, geographically speaking, the western part of Shanghai became dry land 6,000 years ago. The ancient coastline once extended from northwest to southeast, and Shanghai consisted of three areas divided by the Huangpu River and the Wusong River (also named as Suzhou River), which originated from the Taihu Lake and flew through Shanghai. With agreeable climate, abounding products and people living in plenty, Shanghai became a land flowing with milk and honey in the South (South of the river—a region in the lower Yangtze valley, including southern Jiangsu and Anhui and northern Zhejiang). A well-watered place, it naturally became a fishing village and developed the fishery.

Bridges on Suzhou River

World-famous Seaport Shanghai in the
Evening Glow

The water origin of Shanghai could also be verified by other bynames of Shanghai, such as Shen, Chunshen, Sanjiangkou, Hu and Hudu, once all of which were its aliases and some of which carry on being.

It is said that the Huangpu River was canalized by Huang Xie, namely Monarch Chunshen of Chu State, Warring States (475–221 B.C.), and this is the reason why the river is also called Huangxie River or Chunshen River and thus Shanghai's alias Shen.

Then there were three rivers in Shanghai: the Songjiang River, the Dongjiang River and the Loujiang River, all flowing to the East China Sea. Shanghai is located at the estuary of these three waters and is thus named Sanjiangkou, which means the estuary of three rivers.

"Hu" was originally a fishing gear and "Du" refers to the water flowing into the sea. The ancestors of Shanghai fished here with "Hu" and thus the area of Shanghai has got this byname ever since the Jin State (265–420 A. D.). A rampart named "Hu Du Lei" was once built along the seaport of Shanghai and is believed to be a defensive fort.

The name "Shanghai", however, can be traced back as early as 2,000 years ago, when the upper reaches of the Wusong River were called "Shanghai River" and the lower reaches "Xiahai River". The latter name was gradually cast away while the former name "Shanghai River" continued to be used. Later it was abbreviated to "Shanghai" and it is not until 1267 of the Southern Song Dynasty did "Shanghai" became an official name.

Father River and Mother River

Varieties of waters such as lake, river and sea are always regarded as the "parents" of big cities all over the world, and Shanghai makes no exception.

The Wusong River rushes down from the mist-covered water Taihu Lake and joins the torrential Huangpu River at the lower reaches. With fields accompanying both sides, it leads to the new city zone of Shanghai. Though the Huangpu River has been regarded as the "Mother River" of Shanghai all through the ages, experts believe that the Suzhou River (also named Wusong River) is the actual "Mother River". Well then, let's call the Huangpu River the "Father River" for the very moment. Anyhow, Shanghai is the child gestated by both the Suzhou River and the Huangpu River.

Huangpu River——a Real Gold Channel

Fourteen kilometres long, the Huangpu River flows through the downtown area of Shanghai and, as the last anabranch of the Yangtze River, it finally enters there. The Huangpu River nurtures generations of Shanghai people, it is not only the drinking water of all the Shanghainese, but also the gateway that connects Shanghai with the outside world.

Huangpu River Flows into the Sea

Join of Huangpu River and Suzhou River

Approximately the Huangpu River took shape in the Ming Dynasty. In the second year of the reign of Emperor Yongle (1404), Mr. Xia Yuanji, Minister of the Board of Revenue and Population, gave the order to dredge the Fanjiabang Creek connecting to the Huangpu River to solve the stagnation of the Wusong River. Thus the watercourse came into being since then. Because of its yellow sandiness, the watercourse was described in the ancient poem of Ming Dynasty as "a yellow dragon winding in the moonlight" and therefore, it is also called the "Yellow Dragon River".

The Huangpu River is about 500 meters wide and 12 meters deep averagely. A natural harbor, it has even riverbed, wide riverway and calm currents. If we say the more than 10,000 kilometers winding coastline of China looks like a bow and the Yangtze River an arrow, the Shanghai harbor fostered by the Huangpu River is exactly located on the fulcrum of this bow and arrow. Nature-favored geographical position makes the harbor the largest in China and one of the most important ones in the world.

The Suzhou River was originally called the Wusong River. The British businessmen who first came to China called it "the river leading to Suzhou City" for it's the direct way to Suzhou, the famous silk center in the South. Little by little, people carried on using the name "Suzhou River" and abandoned the term "Wusong River".

In the Tang Dynasty, the Wusong River was 20 *li* (a Chinese unit of length: 1 *li* = 500 meters) wide, even wider than today's Yangtze River. In former days, the estuary of Wusong River connected directly with the Yangtze River and the East China Sea. Today, the estuary of the Huangpu River, however, is still called "Wusong Estuary" instead of "Huangpu Estuary", showing that the Wusong River's far more important than the Huangpu River in the old days as well as in modern times.

The great history of the Suzhou River has been vividly recorded in the bridges bestriding over it, and the most well-known one is called *Waibaidu* Bridge. With all these bridges, the Suzhou River strings together the Nanjing Road, the Bund and the Hongkou District, presenting a romantic combination of Chinese and Western urban scenery.

Nanpu Bridge & Yangpu Bridge   Nanpu Bridge and Yangpu Bridge are two famous bridges expanding over the Huangpu River. Nanpu Bridge was built in October 1991 with a length of 8,346 meters, a main span of 423 meters and a width of 30.35 meters. An H-shaped kingtower was set up at each end of the bridge and rises 154 meters high. At each

Nanpu Bridge (1991)—First Bridge on the Huangpu River

Yangpu Bridge (1993)

anchor pier there is a view area of 50 meters high, from where you can take an elevator and enjoy the views. A cable-stayed suspension bridge, it consists of 180 cables with the longest being 227 meters.

Yangpu Bridge was built in 1993 and is 7,654 meters in length and 220 meters in height. With the main span of 602 meters, it is the longest cable-stayed suspension bridge consisting of 256 cables (32 pairs), with the longest being 330 meters. It has view sidewalks and sight-seeing elevators, from where you can enjoy the beautiful scenes along the Huangpu River.

Century-old Waibaidu Bridge——Shanghai's Symbol View

Waibaidu Bridge Built in 1855, the Waibaidu Bridge expanding over the Huangpu River has gone through a century-long history and is regarded as one of the symbols of Shanghai. In 1907, the government rebuilt this wooden bridge into a steel one with two arches and a length of 106.7 meters.

Remarkable Place Fostering Outstanding People

People always say that a remarkable place can produce outstanding people, and Shanghai is such a place from of old. Groups of renowned literators and scholars have appeared in the near-one-thousand-year history of Shanghai, such as Lu Ji, the litterateur and critic of the Western Jin Dynasty; Gu Yewang, the artist of the Southern Dynasties; Wang Xin, the historiographer of the Ming Dynasty; and Dong Qichang, the famous painter and calligrapher. While two world-recognized giant figures, who made great

Lady Huang's Temple

contributions to the economic and cultural development in China, should certainly be Lady Huangdao Po, the primogenitor of spinning, and Xu Guangqi, the pioneer of science and technology.

Lady Huang lived in the late period of the Yuan Dynasty and came from a place called Wunijing, Songjiang area of old Shanghai. Low-born and unbearable to the life of a child bride, she went to Yazhou of Hainan Island by boat and lived there for 30 years. She learned the spinning and weaving techniques from the local residents of Li nationality. Coming back to the hometown in her late years, she combined the techniques with her abundant experience and invented the three-pedal spinning wheel and greatly accelerated the work efficiency. Since then, the cotton cloth from Wunijing has started enjoying such repute that buyers have poured in like continuous streams from all directions. The economy of this area bloomed and it became a textile center. Memorial temples were built after her death in her hometown, Jiading, Chuansha, Fengxian, etc. She was buried in the Dongwan Village of Longhua Town, and the Memorial Temple of Lady Huang built in the Qing Dynasty is located in the Shanghai Arboretum.

Xu Guangqi was an outstanding politician, scientist as well as pioneer of Chinese and Western culture exchange of Shanghai. He lived in the Ming Dynasty and his birthplace still exists today, that is, No. 236 Qiaojia Road,

Lady Huang's Ancestral Temple

Xu Guangqi and Matteo Ricci

Shanghai, which was locally named "Nine-Room-Building" and which is now identified as the "Former Residence of Xu Guangqi". He went to school at seven and at the age of 20, when he was entitled *Xiu Cai* (one who passed the imperial examination at the county level in the Ming and Qing Dynasties), he came back to his hometown and started his teaching career. Meanwhile, he helped his father with his orchard and learned a lot about agriculture, laying a good foundation for his future work *Agricultural Treatise*. He became a successful candidate in the highest imperial examinations at the age of 43 and assumed the office as high as the imperial scholar. With domestic trouble and foreign invasion in the Ming Dynasty, Xu Guangqi found it difficult to achieve a lot in official career and thus devoted his life to scientific research. In those days, men of insight including Xu Guangqi were greatly influenced by the religion and science brought to China by the Western missionaries, and they decided to benefit mankind by science. As a prolific scientist, Xu Guangqi left the world a large number of great works about astronomy, calendric system, irrigation, planting and stockbreeding. Besides his magnum opus *Agricultural Treatise*, he co-translated with the Italian missionary Matteo Ricci the monumental scientific works such as *Geometry*, *Pythagorean Theorem and Hydrology*, revised the calendar, and compiled the *Chongzhen Almanac* of great historical significance. Xu Guangqi died in Beijing and his coffin was carried back to Shanghai later and buried in today's Guangqi Park on Nandan Road. Many places are named after Xu Guangqi and his family and have continued to be used up to the present. For example, today's Xujiahui, literarily means "gathering of the Xu Family", got its name because most offspring of Xu Guangqi inhabit this region.

Memorial Archway in front of Xu Guangqi's Tomb

A-Hundred-Year-Old "Oriental Paris" Shines

Great changes have continuously taken place in Shanghai and the image of a small fishing village has gradually faded away in the history. In the Yuan Dynasty, people living in the north moved to the south for its convenient waterway transportation, and the economic center also moved to the south. Grains were transported to the north through Shanghai, showing its significance as a seaport. The year 1292 made Shanghai a county subordinate to the Songjiang Government. The wall along today's Zhonghua Road and Renming Road near the Town God Temple of Nanshi District is a telling witness of the foundation of the county of Shanghai, which was a middle developed county in those

Intendant of Circuit and County Officials in Ancient Shanghai

days. However, it was left far behind by the flourishing Songjiang, which was wealthy enough to foster all mankind, as well as Suzhou, Hangzhou and Yangzhou, all of which were already prosperous big cities at that time. Nevertheless, Shanghai benefited from its nature-favored geographical position and surpassed the formers later. In the Qing Dynasty, mountain pass and customs house were built in Shanghai, governing the precinct ranging from Lianyungang in the north to Zhejiang in the south and promoting Shanghai to a more important economic status. At the same time, the population of Shanghai has risen a lot in the Ming and Qing Dynasties, from less than 200,000 to 1,000,000. After the ban on maritime trade was abolished, Shanghai opened its arms to the outside world and accelerated its pace of development. With thousands of trading boats coming and going, it gradually became a prosperous city in the southeast of China. Unfortunately the prosperity was damaged in the following war-ridden years and with the expansion of the city zone, we can no longer see a trace of the boom of the former days. Only from the damaged range of the ancient city wall at today's Dajing Road can people vaguely see the charm and glory of old Shanghai. The Dajing Building was set up at the site of this wall, bringing Shanghai another kind of historical scene.

Ancient City Walls at Dajing Building

Guandi Temple——Symbol of Shanghai's
Old Town

Terminus of the Ancient the Board of Works

The year 1843 was a milestone in the history of Shanghai. It witnessed the declaration of opening of Shanghai's ports to the outside world by the first General Consul of Britain. He required the Shanghai Government to mark off an area for them to rent and build up houses, and this is the beginning of concessions, namely foreign settlements. Along with the British concession's appearnce, many other countries advanced such requirements one after another, such as France and the United States. Today's areas like Nanjing Road, the Bund, People's Square, Huaihai Road, the Jing'an Temple and Xujiahui Commercial Zone were all within concessions in those days.

The concessions formed a small capitalistic society within the Chinese feudal society through dit-tats. However, they introduced the comparatively standardized economic competition mode and advanced modern management system. People got to know such terms as finance, bank, and insurance that they never heard of before, and their life was greatly changed with the instalment of electricity, gas, telephone and drainage. Impersonally speaking, the appearance of concessions accelerated the modernization of Shanghai and enlightened a group of intellectuals like Kang Youwei, Liang Qichao and Sun Yat-sen. It is from the concessions that they got to know capitalism and had the idea to reform the old China.

Another significance of the year 1843 is that it's the beholder of the great immigrations, which are the vitals for Shanghai's development. The outskirts

of Shanghai were originally farmlands and fields dotted with some small villages. With the development of modern industries, people replaced hand-loomed cloth with machine-woven cloth, oil lamps with electric lights, and street vendors with department stores. The south occupied a large area but had a small population, and such booming development required a large amount of capital and labour force, whereupon a flock of immigrants poured into Shanghai like continuous streams from other provinces and regions within and without China. One force that cannot be ignored at that time is the incomers from abroad, which has already amounted to 150,000 at that time. They introduced into Shanghai the Western culture like music, ballet, and drama, making their particular contributions to the unique multi-culture of Shanghai. In long-term combination of Chinese and Western cultures, the inimitable Shanghai Culture gradually came into being.

Unique Mixture of East and West

Within its almost-one-hundred-year history, Shanghai glistens in the east like a bright oriental pearl and becomes a great metropolis second to none in the Far East. This metropolis infested with foreign adventurists blends different cultures and wins the crown of Oriental Paris.

China's No. 1s in Shanghai

No. 1 Railway After the first Opium War, the British businessmen in Shanghai asked the Chinese government for agreement to build a railway in Shanghai but were refused. In 1865, the Jardine Matheson Co. founded Wusong Railway Company and started laying the roadbed from Shanghai to Wusong. On February 14th, 1876, a loaded train named Pioneer roared over more than 1 *li*, leaving the Shanghai people astounded and their ears tingle. On March 28th, 1904, the Huning Railway (from Shanghai to Nanjing) was open to traffic and the Huhang (from Shanghai to Hangzhou) was finished in June 1909.

British Mail Cart

No. 1 Post Office Mails used to be a very important means of communication. As early as the time Shanghai opened its port to foreign ships, the Great Britain Steamer Company already had a monthly mail steamer sailing back and forth between Britain and Shanghai, and the day August 10th, 1850 remembers the first arrival of the mail steamer in Shanghai. Eleven years later, the Great Britain Mail House came into existence, commencing the initial stage of post office. In 1878, a Britisher named Howard, director of customs tariff in those days, founded the first post office and, for the first time in history, put on sale stamps. He was entitled post master by the Chinese government of the Qing Dynasty, monopolizing the customs and post office. And the first post office of

First Post Office in Shanghai

China, namely the General Post Office of Qing Dynasty was established at the backyard of the Shanghai Customs Building.

No. 1 Elevator In 1902, an elevator exported from Britain was installed in the Russo-Asiatic Bank (today's Huasheng Building), announcing the first appearance of elevator in China.

No. 1 Tap Water The first waterworks in Shanghai was co-established in 1880 (the 6th year of Guangxu Reign of the Qing Dynasty) by Jardine Matheson Co. and several other foreign firms in the name of the Board of Works. Cast-iron tubes and other equipment were purchased from Britain, and water supply commenced on June 29th, 1883. As Mr. Li Hongzhang pressed the starting gear, Shanghai people welcomed the days with high-quality tap water and said farewell to the river water purified by alum.

No. 1 Car In 1901, the Hungarian doctor Leinz came to Shanghai with two cars for convenience of visiting his patients at home. In those days, Shanghai people were astonished at their shape and speed.

First Telephone in Shanghai

No. 1 Trolley Bus The first trolley bus was put into traffic on March 5th, 1908, indicating the start of modern public transportation in Shanghai. The bottle-green wooden bus started at the Jing'an Temple, passed through the Nanjing Road and terminated on the Bund.

Ancient Trolley Bus on Nanjing Road

No. 1 Park With the establishment of the Garden Bridge (Wai Bai Du Qiao), a park with three sides bordering on the Huangpu River gradually came into being though originally it was a silt shoal. The construction got started in 1866 and was finished in two years. However, this serene park on the Bund once suffered the humiliation of the remark "No Entry for Chinese and Dogs" by the colonists.

No. 1 Film In 1896 (the 22nd year of Guangxu Reign of the Qing Dynasty), a business tycoon named Xu Run, a native Cantonese, showed the Western film in his private garden called "Another Village" for the first time with the aim to liven things up. This is the first time in the history of public film shows. Chinese film commenced its history from 1919 and 1920, with Mr. Zhang Shichuan founded the Star Company and shot the film "Orphan Rescues Grandparents", and Mr. Du Yu founded the Shanghai Company and shot the film "Dead Well Comes Alive".

No. 1 Bank In February 1848, a branch of the London-based Oriental Bank was set up in Shanghai, announcing its first appearance.

No. 1 Gas Lamp In October 1865, the Shanghai Gas Co., Ltd produced the first gas lamp and on December 18 of the same year, gas lamps were installed along Nanjing Road, lightening the night Shanghai ever since.

No. 1 Telephone The first telephone appeared in Shanghai in February 1883 and was transliterated according to Chinese *Pin Yin* as "De Lv Feng". The City life of Shanghai has taken a great step forward with the appearance of telephone.

No. 1 Gramophone The first gramophone was introduced into Shanghai by a British firm in 1897 and it was called "talking machine". Spontaneously the discs were called "singing records".

No. 1 Department Store In 1914, the first department store in Shanghai Sincere Co., Ltd. opened for business on Nanjing Road. Full of beautiful things in eyes, the customers enjoyed for the first time the pleasure of modern shopping. Later, another three department stores opened one after another, namely Wing On Department Store, Xinxin Department Store and Daxin Department Store. They became the four most famous department stores in Shanghai and Daxin Department Store was the predecessor of today's Shanghai No.1 Department Store, soul of the commercial Nanjing Road.

European Gas Lamp

A city's cosmopolitanism is most apparent in its buildings and Shanghai is no different. As the saying goes, architecture is concretionary music. Buildings are the annals of the world. When music and legends keep silent, they keep telling permanence. Buildings in Shanghai also show its history. Shikumen houses (stone gatehouses) are Shanghai's indigenous urban architectural feature, and they are the remains of old Shanghai and express its people's genuine life. Old houses in Shanghai are the most amazing chapter in Shanghai's history. Without them, Shanghai is no longer Shanghai. Shanghai boasts an amazing spread of architectural designs and each holds its own tales and history. More than 1,400 old buildings with a variety of architectural styles are the most vivid and telling faces of Shanghai, tracking down the ghosts of the past.

Longtangs and *Shikumen* Buildings, Shanghai's Major Indigenous Urban Architectural Feature

Shikumen: A Scroll of Common Daily Life

Shikumen (stone gateway) is to Shanghai what *Hutong* is to Beijing, both worthy of the title of representative of their respective folk dwelling houses.

Shikumen, which was popular in last century, has emerged from the womb of *sanheyuan* or *siheyuan*, a compound with houses around a triangle or square courtyard. The entrance with a stone doorframe, black-painted door planks and a pair of giant bronze knockers is typical of traditional folk residence of the South and, as a matter of fact, is the literal meaning of the name *Shikumen*. Like the European architecture, *Shikumen* buildings stand in rows with stone carvings of Western designs on the outer walls and some detail drawings, housing the common Shanghai civilians. Chinese architectural elements are also widely adopted, such as lattice doors and windows and wooden balustrades.

Fish-scale-like tiles of red or black cover the roof of the *Shikumen* buildings and the windows are usually enlaced with liana plants. Two black creaky doors stand tall and upright, warding off evil spirits and keeping out the hurly-burly of the outside world. Although each inch of land in Shanghai is like gold, the residents still grow some plants or keep pets like goldfish, puppy or kitten, enjoying their life in the small dooryard.

Between rows of *Shikumen* buildings there are lines of alleys with archways at both ends, which are called *longtang* in Shanghai. *Longtang* tells vividly the ordinary life of Shanghai civilians day after day and summer is the season when it presents thoroughly the living scene. Men put together several square stools as the dinner table in the dooryard or even in the alley outside the gateway, and neighbours well in with each other have dinner at the same table, sharing dishes.

Shikumen has always been an important stage where various life stories take place. It is a place recording realities in life as birth, marriage and procreation. As people say where you are from shows what you are, habitants of *Shikumen* are quite different from those living in *Siheyuan* of Beijing (a compound with houses around a square coutyard), *Diaojiaolou* (suspended building) of Hu'nan Province, or imposing

Shikumen—the Most Vivid and Telling Faces of Shanghai

Door Details of *Shikumen* Buildings

Carvings of Frontispiece

dwellings and spacious courtyards (a compound of deep, spacious quadrangles one leading into another, usu. occupied by single wealthy family in the old days). In a way, it is *Shikumen* that builds the characters of Shanghainese.

Original *Shikumen* complex are rarely seen now, and those few dotted among the modern skyscrapers, with age-old door planks and exquisite carvings on stone doorcases and doorheads, are by no means inferior. The carving decoration is as delicate as the European basso-relievo, and combines harmoniously with the Chinese elements.

As an indispensable component of Shanghai, *Shikumen* is a must for tourists who want to know real life in this city. Every alley and building is a telling story of the old days.

Horse-shaped Wall

Old Storied Houses: An Old Dream of the Wealthy and Dignitaries

Metropolis infested with foreign adventurists and oriental Paris, this is the image of Shanghai since 1843. With the appearance of concessions, many foreign adventurists came to this feudal imperialistic city with the products that had never been seen by the Shanghainese. In the 1920s, Shanghai became renowned within the Far East and gained names like "Paradise for Adventurers" and "Oriental Paris". Many governors and officials working in Shanghai in those days set up splendent garden houses for personal need. These grand residences usually have green lawns, wandering streams and towering trees, and some are

Delicate Pillars, Porch and Terrace

Exquisite Marble Sculpture

even with tennis court, swimming pool and ballroom. Life in these old storied houses is totally different from that in *Shikumen* buildings. It's nobler, elegant and dainty, as delicate as fine porcelain.

In retrospect, old storied houses have always been telling eyewitnesses of what happened in this metropolis infested with foreign adventurists and oriental Paris. Time brings great changes to these residences, which, just as peerless beauties from eminent families, still get graceful bearings and inner elegance.

Architecture is concretionary music; furthermore, it is concretionary history. Old storied houses in Shanghai are the reflection of an essential phase of Chinese modern history. Even from the architectural perspective, they are the cream of the architecture circles with their aesthetic charm.

Old storied houses are of various styles: British, French, Germanic, Russian, Italian, Spanish, Portuguese and Northern European. With pure interior and exterior decoration, they are of great aesthetic value.

Unique Wooden Structure

Phoenix-tree-covered House

Morriss Garden (today's Ruijin Hotel), No. 118 Ruijin Road Towering camphor trees, emerald lawns, running fountain with marble angel, and four buildings constitute this 48,000 sq. m. grand garden as well as home of Mr. Morriss Jr., son of Mr. Morriss who was an adventurer from Britain and later became director of the Horse Race Committee in those days. He made a fortune in horse racing and his son, after the inheritance, built this garden. The acreage under construction amounts to 1,335 sq. m. Confronted with teak wooden floor, marble columniation and exquisite carvings on the stairs, visitors will feel themselves as if in the midst of a splendent villa in the suburbs of England.

Details of Morriss Garden

Morriss Garden

Chapiter of the Little White House

Former Residence of Chief Director of the French Concession Government (today's Shanghai Arts & Crafts Research Institute), No. 79 Fenyang Road Like a palace of the French Renaissance, this garden residence is full of grandness and elegance with wide stairs leading from both sides to the hall on the second floor, a marble fountain, a broad lawn, the white building with a column jutting out like an arc, a capacious terrace, delicate balustrades and columniation.

Shanghai Arts and Crafts Research Institute——A French Renaissance Garden House Reputed as "the Little White House"

Dingxiang Garden

Dingxiang Garden, No. 849 Huashan Road Dingxiang Garden used to be home of Li Hongzhang's concubine and now is one of the best-preserved garden residences in Shanghai. The main building is a villa of British rustic style with two terraces and corridors with wooden columns of red and white. Chinese elements such as pavilions, rockeries and streams are adopted more frequently.

Chinese Courtyard of Dingxiang Garden

Details of No. 40 Tianping Road

Wenyi Hospital, No. 40 Tianping Road This Spanish-style garden building is the former residence of Zhang Shuxun, a wealthy native from Nanxun, Zhejiang Province. With delicate balconies, exquisite pillars and overlapping grassland, it once housed two national treasures, namely *Dake Ding* and *Dayu Ding* (both ancient cooing vessels), which were contributed by Pan Dayu (offspring of Pan Zuyin, who was Minister of the Board of Works and a famous collector of the late Qing Dyanasty).

Spanish-style Garden Building at No. 40 Tianping Road

Moller House (today's Hengshan Villa), No. 30 South Shanxi Road Former residence of British Jew Mr. Moller, this is the most exquisite and typical one among more than one thousand garden houses in Shanghai. Like all the other Western adventurers coming to Shanghai with the dream of fortune, Mr. Moller came to Shanghai in 1919 without anything. After getting rich through horse racing, he invested in dockyard, customs application, importing and transporting and became a man with great power. The steep roof with pointed windows shows it's of the architectural style of Northern Europe and was originally aiming to accelerate the snow melting in that cold area. It is said this building was set up according to the dream of Mr. Moller's little daughter: the house of Princess Snow White. The house was luxuriously decorated with exquisitely engraved banisters and fine crystalline pendant lamps, and in the garden there's a bronze horse statue modeled on Mr. Moller's "Exploit Hero", the horse that helped him to make the first fortune.

Bronze Horse in Moller

Northern-European-Style Moller

Liu's Garden (today's Shanghai Writers Association), No. 675 Jvlu Road Former residence of Mr. Liu Jisheng (junior brother of Liu Hongsheng, who was in those days the Coal Magnate, Match Magnate and Cement Magnate of China), this classical European style building was built in 1930 and boasts majestic Romanesque columns, exquisite cockle stairs, the artistic West Hall with fine engraved glass ornament, the Grand Hall with tremendous crystalline pendant lamps, and the splendid fountain with the marble statue of Cupid transported from Italy.

Cupid's Sculpture at No. 675 Jvlu Road

No. 675 Jvlu Road, Former Liu's Garden

Sassoon Villa (today's Hainan Zhidi Industrial Co., Ltd.), No. 2310 Hongqiao Road Former residence of a British businessman named Sassoon Victor, the Magnate of Real Estate who possessed the Sassoon Mansion (today's Peace Hotel), Hamilton House (today's Fuzhou Building) and many other famous constructions, this typical British style villa is located in western Shanghai and boasts the irregular layout, wide lawns, running creams, the brick-and-wood-framework, the steep red roof, and the British style chimney. After the liberation, it was used as the infirmary for the employees of the textile industry.

Old storied houses are an important chapter in Shanghai's modern history and this a fundamental course for the people who want to know Shanghai. Like the main blood vessel of Shanghai's historical civilization, they bestow Shanghai sanguinity and charm.

Sassoon Villa

Former Residences of Celebrities: Authentic Records of Influential Figures

Shanghai has always been the stage where influential figures give full play to their talents and fulfill their great ambitions.

Many celebrities used to control this stage now have passed away, leaving nothing but their residences telling fragmentary anecdotes and witnessing the great changes of the world.

Sun Yat-sen's Former Residence   Sun Yat-sen's Former Residence is located on 7 Xiangshan Road, which is densely shadowed by phoenix trees. This carmine Spanish style garden house was given to Mr. Sun Yat-sen as a gift by an overseas Chinese businessman from *Nanyang* (an old name for the Malay Archipelago, the Malay Peninsula and Indonesia or for Southeast Asia). It is in this house that Mr. Sun Yat-sen spent six years from 1918 to 1924; probed into the cooperation issue of the Communist party and the Kuomintang with Li Dazhao, one of the founders of the Communist Party; met the envoy of the Soviet Union, Lin Boqv, and Zhu

Sun Yat-sen's Former Residence

De; and brewed the strategy of uniting Communist Party with the Soviet Union and the New Three People's Principles.

Now what displayed in the house are the things that have once been used by Mr. Sun Yat-san, such as his desk with the four treasures of study: brush, ink stick, ink slab and paper, his sofa, tea table, and clothes rack. Today, visitors come here from all over the world to commemorate this giant of history.

Song Qingling's Former Residence

Song Qingling's Former Residence   Built in 1920, this building at the intersection of Middle Huaihai Road and Wukang Road became home of Song Qingling from 1948. The garden of camphor trees on the east is particularly nice and provides green shades all the year round. The lawn under the southern window attracts groups of pigeons coming and looking for food.

Song Qingling's former bedroom and office upstairs exhibit pictures of her with her husband Dr. Sun Yat-sen and her marriage portion. Other highlights include the sitting room, the study and the dining room where Song met many national leaders and distinguished guests. The gifts presented by their foreign friends and about 5,000 books are displayed here.

Zhou Enlai's Former Residence

Zhou Enlai's Former Residence   Zhou Enlai's former residence is located on Sinan Road. It boasts the slope roof with red tiles, cobble-decorated outer walls wrapped with ivy, and the hypaethral stairs connecting the balcony directly to the garden with towering bushy trees. With the disguise of Zhou Enlai's residence, it had once worked as the Shanghai Office of the Central Committee of the Communist Party of China. It is in this house that Zhou Enlai held press conferences, banqueted democrats, met General Marshall, and worked on the cooperation of the Communist Party and the Kuomintang.

Zhang Xueliang's Former Residence

Zhang Xueliang's Former Residence   Zhang Xueliang's former residence is located on Gaolan Road. This is a white Spanish style house with a small but exquisite garden dotted with camphor trees and magnolia trees. General Zhang Xueliang lived here in 1934 with his wife Zhao Yidi and their only son. This quiet place witnessed him talking with people with lofty ideals about resistance against the Japanese invaders and saving the nation, and gestating the Xi'an Incident.

Former Residence of Jiang Jieshi and Song Meiling

Lu Xun's Former Residence

Former Residence of Jiang Jieshi and Song Meiling The former residence of Jiang Jieshi and Song Meiling, a land of eternal peace far from the madding crowd, is located on Dongping Road. It is a French style house with fish-scale-like red tiles, nicely strewed chimney and sky windows, and arched door and porch. On December 12, 1927, Jiang Jieshi and Song Meiling got married in Shanghai and this house became their bridal chamber. It is said that both of them liked the house very much, and Song Meiling, the first lady of China at that time, elaborated on the decoration and often met friends and guests there.

Lu Xun's Former Residence Lu Xun, a pioneer of the Chinese New Culture Movement, is the litterateur who used vernacular Chinese first in his writing. His incisive and piquant style of writing anatomized the tortured and depressive nation like a scalpel. The image *Ah Q* in one of his novels is widely known in China. After the Great Revolution failed, he dedicated the rest of his life to the Left-wing Cultural Movement.

Lu Xun's former residence is located on Shanyin Road. It is a three-story building shadowed in bushy trees: the first floor worked as the living room and dining room; the second floor used to be his workroom and bedroom; and the third floor served as his son Zhou Haiying's bedroom and the guest room.

Huangpu River

The Bund: Magnificent Living-Room of Shanghai

The Bund (*Waitan* in Chinese) is the most famous in Shanghai. People compare it to the living room of Shanghai because it's a boastful reminder of the city's most beautiful and majestic facet. Today it is the first place to which all visitors to Shanghai head. Even Shanghai people love to take strolls on the Bund and enjoy the great view there.

Originally a bottomland of the Huangpu River, the Bund gets it Anglo-Indian name from the embankments built up to discourage flooding. The British developed it into concession and gave the name "the Bund", meaning the street running along the river.

Since then, Shanghai boomed rapidly and 52 grand buildings of different style appeared along this 1.5km from the Garden Bridge (*Wai Bai Du Qiao*) on the north to East Jinlin Road on the south, combining harmoniously with each other and composing a classical architectural symphonic poem.

Its bay-like shape distinguishes the Bund from any straight streets: always-panoramic scenery of all the architecture. An architectural expo, the Bund portrays the semi-feudal and semi-colonial China and is seen as the epitome of Shanghai's modern history.

Architecture Complex on the Bund

← Exquisite Dome,
Columns and Frescos of HSBC

No. 12 is the grandest building on the Bund, the former Hong Kong and Shanghai bank (HKSB). It was established to finance trade and soon became one of the richest and most powerful foreign banks in Shanghai. The British boasted that it was "the finest building east of Suez", featuring the lofty marble columns, the beautiful mosaic ceiling, the delicate carving the gate, and the twelve zodiac signs. The bronze lions once guarded the entrance can now be found the Shanghai History Museum.

Bronze Lion at HSBC

Bronze Lion and HSBC

Peace Hotel and the Bank of China

No. 19 is the Peace Palace Hotel (1906), one of the oldest buildings on the Bund. It is a building in the style of British Renaissance.

Opposite is the famous Peace Hotel (former Sassoon Mansion) at No. 20. This thirteen-story building was once the most luxurious hotel in the Far East and is still an Art-Deco masterpiece. With the front elevation in the shape of an "A", it boasts the dark-green pyramidal roof 19 meters high and the majestic decorations.

The imposing Bank of China building, at No. 23, was the only one designed by a Chinese architect. It was built in 1937 with the specific instructions that it should not be higher than the

Interior of Peace Hotel

Former Merchants Bureau on the Bund

adjacent Sassoon Mansion. The building is a strange architectural mish-mash with inscriptions decoration-engraved Chinese character "壽" (meaning longevity), traditional Chinese style baluster and window ornaments, and a blue Chinese roof made of glazed tiles and *dougong* (wooden square blocks inserted between the top of a column and a crossbeam in Chinese architecture).

No. 27 is the former Jardine Matheson Co., the overlord in trading business in those days. It was built in 1920 under the design of a British named Wilson with enormous granite and steels from the United States, and got finished six years later. The frontispiece consists of two copper-coated gates and four ornate steel windows on both sides. At each corner inside the building, there is a Roman style statue. However, most of these art pieces are damaged. Now the building serves as the Foreign Trade Building.

Roam on the Bund, the magnificent living room from where you get to know Shanghai.

Jardine, Matheson & Co., Ltd

Details of Jardine, Matheson & Co., Ltd

Views of a city are like a floating scroll of paintings. Only by wandering down the streets can one appreciate thoroughly the beauty and charm of the city. As an international metropolis, Shanghai boasts hundreds of busy business streets and quiet interlaced sidewalks that constitute a grand symphony. A stroll around the city can reveal different scenes and tales. Therefore, let's take a stroll and experience the city.

New Bund with a New Look

In the eyes of Shanghai people, the Bund is a symbol and their eternal pride no matter what changes time may bring to Shanghai. The comprehensive reconstruction project of the narrow and crowded old Bund started in 1992 and brought a brand-new look: broadened road extends in all directions and presents busy tourist traffic; greenbelts dress the city with plants and flowers; the

Lovers' Wall on the Bund

Chen Yi's Statue

Basso-relievos Decoration

statue of Chen Yi, first mayor of Shanghai, overlooks the Chen Yi Square at one end of Nanjing Road; the Theme Square "Pace of the Times" opposite to the customhouse tells the different hours in various cities with its water columns of the waterfall clock; the artistic carving wall of basso-relievos against the building of Hong Kong & Shanghai Banking Corporation (HSBC) embodies the theme "Yesterday, Today and Tomorrow" as well as "Power, Wisdom and Courage"; six columns on East Yan'an Road and the eighty-year-old observatory constitute the sight named "For Tomorrow"; a waterfall 25 meters wide and 3 meters high highlights the "Light of the Huangpu River" River

Art Wall on the Bund

Cruise Square; and a sculpture complex with the theme of "Master of the Earth" at Xinkaihe Road terminates the scenic line of the Bund.

The grand Bund has hosted hundreds of concerts and performances given by famous singers, musical instrument players, children amateurs and foreign bands as well as regular public activities such as music, painting, calligraphy and dancing. A continuous stream of audience comes here and participates in these comfortable and lively activities which endow Shanghai with a distinctive culture of superb taste.

← Meteorological Signal Station on the Bund

No. 1 Bay of Shanghai

The Lovers Wall on the Bund used to be a hotspot for people in love. Pairs of sweethearts leaning against the riverside wall and whispering to each other formed a special scene of the Bund and attracted many foreign journalists who reported this in the overseas newspapers. Although the Lovers Wall is no longer in existence, the Bund keeps being a best choice of the young lovers.

Sightseeing Tunnel connecting the Bund and the Oriental Pearl TV Tower, the Sightseeing Tunnel extends 646.70 meters long and can send the passengers from one side to the other within five minutes. It adopts high-tech equipment and provides a fantastic view.

Sightseeing Tunnel on the Bund →

Wall Street of the Far East

Before the Opium War, there's no bank in the modern sense in China. People withdrew and deposited money at qianzhuang (old-style Chinese private bank) or *piaohao* (exchange shop). After Shanghai became a prosperous commercial port, however, the financial activities brisked up rapidly. The first bank was established on the Bund in 1847, with that about ten more were set up one after another. All of them were branches of British, Japanese, French, German, Russian or American banks. In 1879, Mr. Sheng Xuanhuai founded the first Chinese bank - China Trade Bank. Since then, the China Central Bank, Bank of China, Bank of Communications and Agricultural Bank of China ascended to the stage. The 1920s and the 1930s are the golden ages of financial industry in Shanghai and the Bund became the financial center of China and within the Far East. Within an area of no more than 1 sq. km., the Bund boasted 113 banking buildings holding more than 180 financial institutions and connecting with the financial networks within and outside the country. Shanghai's economy was far ahead of big cities of the Far East such as Hong Kong and Tokyo.

In the 1990s, the world economic development center has been transferred to Asia and the Pacific and Shanghai has met a good opportunity to re-establish its status as an international financial center. Among all the foreign banks

← The National City Bank of New York
(CITIBANK)

Pudong Development Bank

about 70 % are on the world top 50 list. That the National City Bank of New York (CITIBANK) founded in 1812 moved its headquarters in China from Hong Kong to Shanghai has attracted worldwide attention. Hundreds of skyscrapers sprouting out in the Lujiazui Finance & Trade Development Zone in Pudong extend the Financial Street along the Bund, composing the Wall Street of the Far East.

Pudong: A Resplendent Oriental Pearl

The area directly across from the Bund is the Pudong New Area, which occupies 523 sq. km. and consists of the entire eastern bank of the Huangpu River. Geographically, it is the intersection area of an Gold Watercourse and an Gold Coast, namely the Huangpu River and the East China Sea. With the announcement of the reform and opening up policy, it has become China's economic powerhouse, a hotspot drawing attentions from all over the world.

Public Park at Lujiazui Finance and Trade Zone

Skyscrapers in Greenbelts The most impressive feature distinguishing Pudong New Area is its harmonious combination of human being and nature, with greenbelts extending in all directions in the midst of the skyscrapers sprouting out of the ground.

Lujiazui Central Park, a green gem inlaid in the booming Lujiazui Financial and Commercial Development Zone, occupies an area of 8,600 sq. m. and boasts the man-made lake in the shape of Pudong New Area domain, the wandering paths outlining the magnolia pattern (magnolia is the city flower of Shanghai), modern white sight tents standing in vivid contrast against well-preserved old dwelling houses, the double ringy fountain presenting liquid statues, and 4,000 colorful cyprinoids (*Cyprinus carpio*) from Japan frolicking in the pond.

The Century Avenue, the first scenic road in China, is the most beautiful in the Pudong New Area, ranging from the Oriental Pearl TV Tower on the west to the Century Park on the east and consisting of ten driveways and two sidewalks. The separation greenbelts between the eight main driveways and the two supplement ones are 5.5 meters wide, and the sidewalks, together with the greenbelts, are 46 meters wide. Along the northern sidewalk of the Century Avenue stand eight esplanades that are respectively named after a tree and constitute the China Botanical Gardens. The avenue also boasts two sculpture squares with man-made waterfalls, galleries, paths, bridges and stream, modern metal sculptures, and elaborately designed street lamps.

Century Park

Occupying an area of 140.3 hectares, the Century Park is located at the east end of the Century Avenue. It's the largest ecological city park in Shanghai, consisting of different zones such as forests, lawns, gardens, and avian area. With stretches of bamboo forests connecting the Gingko Avenue, storied parterres, wavy bosks, pleasant beaches and lofty palm trees, it is a beautiful green area in which city inhabitants can enjoy the quiet and escape the concrete jungle. The giant fountain is made up of 323 sprouts, and the water column can reach 80 meters high. Led by the theme of "Ecology and Art", the Century Avenue and the Century Park combine harmoniously the classicality with the modernity, and the east with the west. Like a giant lung of the city, the Century Park gets rid of the stale and takes in the fresh day and night.

Riverside Avenue

Oriental Pearl TV Tower: No. 1 of Asia The 468-meter-high Oriental Pearl TV Tower in Pudong New Area is the No. 1 Tower of Asia and the No. 3 of the world, next to the Toronto TV Tower of Canada and the Moscow TV Tower of Russia. Flanked by the Nanpu Bridge and the Yangpu Bridge, the Oriental Pearl TV Tower becomes a symbol of Shanghai.

It consists of three inclined tubes, three vertical tubes and eleven spheres, forming a giant dimensional frame. Six elevators installed in the tubes can take any of the spheres. The lower sphere has a diameter of 50 meters and serves as the

Oriental Pearl TV Tower

recreation ground with programmes such as Trip-round-the-World, Space Travel, Time Tunnel and Sightseeing Tour. The nine-story upper sphere with a diameter of 45 meters is 263 meters high and composed of the transmission rooms occupying 6 stories and the rotational overlook stand and restaurant taking up 3 stories. The overlook stand with a panoramic view of the beautiful scenes along the Huangpu River can hold 1,600 people at the same time and its rotation takes one hour. The 274-meter-high rotation restaurant has a seating capacity of 500 and boasts fascinating aerial scenery. From the upper sphere, a speed elevator goes directly to the uppermost sphere: a silver space capsule where many summit meetings take place. Between the red upper sphere and lower sphere there are five crossbeams embedded with five smaller spheres with a diameter of twelve meters—the "Hotel of the Air". Each sphere has three stories and five luxury suites.

Revolving Restaurant of the Oriental Pearl TV Tower

The light effect is acclaimed as another acme of perfection. Like a legendary luminous pearl, the Oriental Pearl TV Tower shines in the night sky of Shanghai and enhances each other's beauty with the lights on the grand buildings along the Bund.

Oriental Pearl TV Tower at Night

← Jinmao Tower, Tallest Building in Shanghai

Lofty Skyscrapers What keep sprouting out of land in the Lujiazui Finance and Trade Zone in Pudong are the lofty buildings and towering mansions with the Jinmao Tower as the peak. This silver high-tech skyscraper has 88 stories and adopts the architectural style of traditional Chinese concept of art, both interior and exterior. The stories above 54 constitute the Grand Hyatt, which boasts its 555 rooms all with views. What could be acclaimed as its peak of perfection is the Cloud Nine Bar, whose ceiling is as high as 31 stories. Sitting in the sofa of the bar and looking up, people cannot help marveling at the glaring lights and the infinite space. But if you look down from the top floor of the mansion, the bar seems as fathomless as the bottom of a well with lights like fireflies.

Jinmao Tower

Interior of Jinmao Tower

Shanghai International Convention Center

Now, the Shanghai Global Financial Center, the will-be highest building in the world, is under construction and will be a new symbol of Pudong in the 21st century. It boasts 95 stories, a height of 460 meters and a rooftop with the "Moon Door", a traditional Chinese artistic architectural style.

The Shanghai International Convention Center located on the southeast of the Oriental Pearl TV Tower is another unique architecture. Modern assembly rooms and auditoriums, advanced multi-functional halls, capacious exhibition halls, luxury presidential suites and about three hundred grand business suites, and pleasing entertainment grounds constitute this splendent building. Its grand banqueting hall can hold 3,000 people at the same time and the International Hall could accommodate a conference of eight hundred with simultaneous interpretation equipment of ten different languages. A series of import meetings took place here, including the '99 Fortune Forum, APEC, etc.

Fireworks and Lights

Oriental Art Center The newly-built Oriental Art Center is located on the north of the Century Avenue in Pudong and occupies an architectural area near 40,000 sq. m. It's a design of Paul Andreu, the famous French architect, and consists of five hemispheroids. The building is decorated with ceramic pedants of all colors and over 800 dome lights which will dance elegantly when beautiful music starts.

A series of hi-tech light and sound equipments including the PDA lighting control console and the best sound mixing console of the world help carry out numerous wonderful performances here, such as symphonies, ballets, ice shows, musicals, dramas, etc.

Oriental Art Center becomes another cultural highlight in Shanghai and helps promote China's art creation and popularization.

Oriental Art Center

Shanghai Science and Technology Museum

Science and Future Shanghai Science and Technology Museum, another symbol of Shanghai, is located in the Century Square, the hinterland of Pudong New Area. Occupying a construction area of 96,000 sq. m., it looks like spreading wings ready to take off and onrushing waves chasing each other, symbolizing the progressing development of science. The unique ovate hall occupies a construction area of 70,000 cubic meters and constitutes the "heart" of Shanghai Science and Technology Museum, which is crystallite and glistening at night.

The exhibits in Shanghai Science and Technology Museum are open to the public, who can observe closely and operate personally the exhibits to get a direct experience of the science theories. The layout embodies a fusion of innovative concepts such as heaven and earth, life, wisdom, creativity and future, vividly presenting the evolution of the boundless universe through all ages by breaking the bounds of time. Severn exhibition areas (the Lithosphere Exploration, the Manifestations of Nature, the Wisdom Light, the Children's Science and Technology Garden, the Audiovisual Hall, the Cradle of Designers, and the Nature Museum) and three special cinemas (the Stereoscopic Cinema, the Spheric-screen Cinema and the Four-dimensional or 4-D Cinema) constitute the Shanghai Science and Technology Museum, which, with the theme of "Nature·Human·Science and Technology", provides the visitors with an opportunity to give free rein to their creativity, talents and imagination.

Pudong New Area Government Building

People's Square

People's Square: The Beating Heart of Shanghai

Located in downtown and occupying an area of 140,000 sq. m., the People's Square is the heart of the metropolis Shanghai as well as a political and cultural center.

Great Changes of the Racecourse　The spacious People's Square with the green-shadowed People's Park used to be the largest racecourse in Far East before liberation. In 1861, a British director from the Horse Racing Committee colluded with the British Consul and forced the *Daotai* (formerly, Intendant of Circuit) of Shanghai in those days to plot out a ground for horse racing courses. With the compulsory approval from the incapable local officials, the English rode a horse and delimited with its footprints the area for the racecourse, which occupied an area of 466 *mu* (Chinese unit of area, 1/15 of a hectare) and deprived more than 30,000 farmers of their homes. The racecourse was built in 1862 and soon became a sultry spot for the immigrants living in Shanghai. Horse racing became a great recreational event that attracted a continuous stream of audience. All the time the racecourse was bubbling with cries from all sorts of people, including gentlewomen and

Racecourse of the Past

People's Square at Night

gentlemen, managers of foreign firms, bluejacket and even ruffians. The racecourse sometimes worked as the drill field of the foreign troops or the place for celebration events. During the War of Resistance against Japan (1937–1945), it was used as the barrack of the Japanese army and then the club of American troops.

At the beginning of the liberation, the racecourse, having gone through the swift and great changes of the world, was rebuilt into the People's Avenue, the People's Square and the People's Park. The building used to stand beside the racecourse was rebuilt into Shanghai Library and the stands of the racecourse became a stadium. The noisy gambling-den in former days is now a place where people of Shanghai can gather, entertain themselves and take a rest.

Doves of Peace Hovering over the Sky In recent years, a comprehensive reconstruction has brought a new look to the People's Square: 699-meter-long and 32-meter-wide granite revenue extending straight and far; sideways greenbelts occupying an area of 80,000 sq. m. and, together with the People's Park of 120,000 sq. m., inhaling

Doves at People's Square

the fresh and exhaling the stale like the lungs of Shanghai; a music fountain occupying 320 sq. m. dancing trippingly with glass steps of red, yellow and blue encircled and introducing to its center— the rilievi of Shanghai's domain; Purple copper parterres ornamenting around the fountain and six basso—relievos guarding the four entries—the seal characters of "申" and "滬" (both abbreviated forms of Shanghai), the statuary of Lady Huangdao Po (primogenitor of spinning), the statuary of Xu Guangqi (Pioneer of Science and Technology Exploration in China), the design of friendship and the pattern of peace.

Accompanied by the Rising Sun Square (Xuri Guang Chang) on the east side and the Bright Moon Square (Mingyue Guang Chang) on the west side, People's Square boasts the largest garden square of Shanghai with more than 400,000 trees of different species like camphor trees, deodar cedars, maidenhair trees, magnolia trees and evergreen shrubberies, and welcomes the citizens' sword dancing, shadowboxing, jogging and walking in the early morning every day. On the southeast corner of People's Square there is a dovecote which shelters thousands of white doves of peace. Either strolling and pecking at the square or hovering over the sky, they are an important addition to the amenities of the city.

A Dazzling Night

City Hall: A Political Center   Most of the constructions at People's Square are located on its middle axis and the city hall is situated on the north. This is a stately building with ten stone pillars of nine meters high at the entrance, wide granite-paved walkway introducing to the main hall of seventy two meters high, the granite-coated complex indicating the immutability and grandeur of the authority, the basso-relievos ornament with the pattern of magnolia (Shanghai's City Flower) sprinkles the building with its lively lines and artistic atmosphere.

The interior is equipped with advanced scientific and technological facilities and the intelligentized office automation system. The operation and security of the building are also controlled through computers.

Shanghai Government Building

Shanghai Grand Theatre

Shanghai Grand Theatre: A Palace of Art   On the northwest of the middle axis of People's Square is Shanghai Grand Theatre, a semi-transparent modern art palace of simple and soft lines that occupies an area of 20,000 sq. m. Designed by a French master architect, it boasts most the crown-like roof, a camber arch turning up to the sky, symbolizing the broad and extensive bosom of Shanghai to various cultures and arts of the world. A gigantic abstract oil painting named "Reviving Spirit" is hanging in the front hall; it is a work of Mr. Zhu Dequn, the famous artist residing in France. The Grand Theatre consists of the Lyric Theatre Auditorium, the Middle Theatre Auditorium and the Small Theatre Auditorium, all of which are equipped with top-ranking professional acoustic facilities. All around the year the Lyric Theatre Auditorium hosts international performances like concerts, dances, dramas, operas, etc., presenting visual and acoustical feasts to the people of Shanghai. Every night, the glittering and translucent Grand Theatre draped in resplendent lights turns into a most eye-catching artistic palace.

Shanghai Museum: A Storehouse of Cultural Relics Built according to the traditional Chinese concept of "round Heaven and square Earth", Shanghai Museum is a construction with square foundation and round roof standing on the south of the middle axis of People's Square. It recalls an ancient bronze *ding* (three-legged food vessel used for cooking and serving), and also echoes the shape of a famous gigantic bronze mirror of the Han Dynasty which is exhibited in the museum. Four carved archways have tracked record of the evolution of Chinese culture and history; while eight stone lions and mythological beasts such as *pixie* and *tianlu* of the past dynasties crouching over the entrance vividly reveals the venerable and resplendent Chinese culture.

Occupying a construction area of 38,000 sq. m., Shanghai Museum consists of seven floors with two underground and the other five aground. It is one of the best-equipped museums of China with its advanced Ten-Proof technology, namely quakeproof, lightningproof, fireproof, burglarproof, mothproof, dampproof, dryness-proof, lightproof,

Stone Buddha in Shanghai Museum

Shanghai Museum at Night

dustproof and antipollution. Twelve galleries such as the Ancient Chinese Bronzes Gallery, the Ancient Chinese Sculpture Gallery, the Ancient Chinese Ceramics Gallery, the Chinese Painting Gallery, the Calligraphy Gallery, the Ancient Chinese Jade Gallery, the Coin Gallery, the Ming and Qing Furniture Gallery, the Minority Nationalities Art Gallery, the Seals Gallery, etc. exhibit about 1,000,000 works of art (about 120,000 are collector's items) and more than 200,000 artistic and historical books. In addition to galleries there are also three exhibition halls for temporary displays. The museum adopts the most advanced technology to autocontrol the temperature and humidity for the exhibits and provides visitors audio-guides available in eight languages.

Shanghai Museum has hosted a series of influential exhibitions, including the Exhibition of Art Works of Egypt from the Britain Museum, the Exhibition of Maya Civilization from Mexico, the National Treasures of Chinese Painting and Calligraphy, etc.

Shanghai Museum

Shanghai Urban Planning Exhibition Hall To the east of People Square is another impressive building—Shanghai Urban Planning Exhibition Hall. Standing 43.3 meters high and occupying a building area of 18,393 sq. m., the hall is a distinctive tourist attraction but essentially enjoyable hi-tech propaganda. The exhibits paint a picture of how Shanghai will develop in the next 15 years and the highlight is an absorbing scale plan of Shanghai of more than 600 sq. m. the Information Harbor exhibits Shanghai's recent achievement in electronic commerce, industrial design, city operation, distance education and intellectualized family life. Hi-tech video display and digital movies show the inexhaustible possibilities of future life.

Interior of Shanghai Urban Planning Exhibition Hall

Shanghai Urban Planning Exhibition Hall

Shanghai Concert Hall

Shanghai Concert Hall Originally named Nanjing Theatre, Shanghai Concert Hall was built in 1930 and screened only movies. A resounding success at its appearance, it is equipped with top-ranking facilities and decorated in the classical renaissance style: rufous facing bricks, a magnificent hall, tremendous semicircular windows, a gorgeous portico made of four Ionic pillars and a three-meter-high basso-relievo. Located at an intersection, Shanghai Concert Hall has a facet of 45° facing the corner. Circular stairs start from the vestibule and lead to the lounges and the auditorium, the latter of which is also decorated in the renaissance style and commands fantastic sound effects. It was converted into Shanghai Concert Hall in 1959 and has became a shrine to the classic music lovers.

Columns of Shanghai Concert Hall

The city planning made Shanghai Concert Hall move 66.4 meters southeast and receive a renovation. A brand-new Shanghai Concert Hall seizes the musical fans' hearts with its delicate basso-relievos of Greece myth, the dome made of 200,000 quadrate gold foils (side length of 10 centimeters), the portraits of famous Chinese and Western musicians such as Xian Xinghai, Nie Er, Huang Zi, He Lvting, Ludwig Von Beethoven, Franz Liszt, Franz Schubert, Johannes Brahms and Pyotr Ilyich Tchaikovsky along the hallways, the copies of the manuscripts of Xian Xinghai and Nie Er, and, of course, the melodious music.

Nanjing Road: No. 1 Commercial Street of China

Nanjing Road starts from the Bund on the east and terminates at the intersection of Jing'an Temple and West Yan'an Road on the west. Divided into two parts by Xizang Road, it extends 5.5 kilometers long and traverses 26 streets in downtown.

Extending Road with Honor and Disgrace   The famous Nanjing Road has gone through a history more than 100 years long and full of humiliation and disgrace. With the signing of the Nanjing Treaties, Shanghai served as a treaty port and Nanjing Road became the British Concession and later a public concession. Foreign adventurists abused the land along Nanjing Road by selling opium, opening gambling-dens, plundering land, and dumping goods. Nanjing Road was full of scenes of debauchery. Of course, Nanjing Road has its honor and glory. The famous May 30th Movement (1925) took place on this road.

Nanjing Road of 100 Years Old

After 1949, Nanjing Road has been reconstructed into a most flourishing commercial street of China boasting more than 600 stores with products

Prosperous Nanjing Road of Last Century

ranging from food to clothes. Many of them are century-old stores. In the 1980s, great changes have taken place on Nanjing Road with high buildings sprouting out and shopwindows artistically decorated. Counters were replaced by open shelves, creating a warm and comfortable shopping environment. Worthy of the name of No. 1 Commercial Street of China, it is a must for all the visitors to Shanghai.

Booming "No. 1 Street of China"

Duoyunxuan, a Painting and Calligraphy Supplies Store

Top Fashion with Best Brands The section between North Chengdu Road and Changde Road is called "Nanjing Road in Jing'an" where many important international business activities, external public functions and exhibitions take place.

Shanghai Exhibition Center

Shanghai Exhibition Center Designed by the Soviet Union architect Andreyev, Shanghai Exhibition Center is a typical Russia-style construction and has got several names such as Sino-Russia Amity Mansion and Shanghai Exhibition Hall. It was finished in 1955 and occupies an area of 80,000 sq. m. The construction boasts its huge fountain in the middle of the square, the main building topped with a gold-plated steel tower and the wing buildings stretching backwards. On the top of the tower there is a red star 199 meters high, overlooking the four smaller gold-plated steel towers around. The carving decorations, floors and domes of the center have been repaired and a new roof made of 5 kilograms gold was placed on the roof.

Shanghai Center Alternately named after its American designer John Portman, Shanghai Center is a grand construction 164.8 meters high with a castle-like entrance and spacious courtyard and boasts luxury flats, imposing offices, world-class shopping malls, the five-star Portman Ritz-Carlton Hotel with 6 restaurants of different-style cuisines, bars, swimming pool, gymnasium, indoor tennis court and racket ball court, the business center providing 24 hours service, as well as the multi-functional theatre built according to the prototype of the Marquis Theatre of the Broadway and presenting dramas, operas, symphony concerts and ballets.

Shanghai Center

← Plaza 66

Golden Triangle   The golden triangle on Nanjing Road consists of the Plaza 66, the CITIC Square and the Westgate Mall. It is the fashion center of Shanghai and the first choice of world-famous brands to release their new collections.

With a height if 288 meters, Plaza 66 boasts the highest building in Puxi and from the distance looks like the Times Square of New York. A convergence of Louis Vuitton, Cartier, Dior, etc., it helps Shanghai keep pace with the world fashion trend.

The theme of CITIC Square is internationalization. It has a luxury modern exhibition hall named "Fashion Salon" that has hosted a series of international fashion releases, exhibition fair of world-famous brands and car displays and attracted many conspicuous companies like Motorola, Ford and Wyeth and many foreign institutions to set up their offices here one after another.

Westgate Mall is made up of the office building of 37 stories and the shopping center of 10 stories which boasts the Japanese-style Isetan Department Store, jewelry shops, restaurants of different cuisines, entertainment center and the Studio City, one of the most well-equipped cinemas in Shanghai.

Westgate Mall

Plaza 66

Century-Old Stores Four earliest department stores of China, that is, Wing On, Sincere, Sun Company and Sun Sun Store, are located on the east section of Nanjing Road. At the beginning of the 1800s, founders of these four department stores decided to introduce the Western operation mode into China by setting up commodious stores to replace the vendors. When the Wing On Department Store was opened in 1917, customers found everything they want there: daily necessities on the first floor, woolen and silk cloth on the second floor, and jewelry, watches, clocks and musical instruments on the third floor. Led by these four department stores, Shanghai's consumption industry boomed rapidly.

Wing On Department Store

After liberation, they kept the lead and changed their names respectively into Number One Department Store, Hualian Commercial Building, Shanghai Fashion Company and Shanghai No. 1 Provisions Store. Number One Department Store alone attracts more than 100,000 customers every day and achieves a sale of over 2 billion yuan. Besides the four department stores, there are several other famous stores located there: Shanghai Arts and Crafts Shopping Center has 160 categories and 16,000 types of jewelry, jade articles, ivory carvings, rosewood furniture and artwork; Laofengxiang Jewelry Store founded in 1852 is famous for its purity, design and variety of jewelry; Jingdezhen Porcelain Artware specializes in porcelain and curios;

Shanghai No. 1 Provisions Store (Sun Sun Store)

Duoyunxuan is the most famous painting and calligraphy supplies store dating from 1900; Zhongyi Embroidery Shop sells elaborate works from Jiangsu, Hu'nan, Guangdong and Sichuan. Leiyunshang and Cai Tong De are two well-known Chinese drugstores with the former founded in 1861 and selling medicinal materials such as ginseng and stag antler and the latter established in 1883 and famous for its various medical liquors; Laokafook Silk & Woolen Store is opened in 1860 and is known by silks and satins; Baroman sells and takes order for men's suits; Envol and Pengjie boast women's fashionable dresses; First Fur and Xue Bao are exclusive fur shops; Lantang Shoe Store wins great reputation with lady's shoes and Shengxifu is titled as the "cap world".

Like a century-old tree, Nanjing Road is well established and vigorously developed and worthy of the title of "Shopping Heaven".

Shanghai Fashion Company (Sincere Company)

One Department Store (Sun Company)

Park Hotel, the Tallest Building in the Past in Shanghai

Hotels and Night Scenes   No hotel is more famous than the Park Hotel on Nanjing Road. Built in 1934 under the design of Hungarian architect Ladislaus Edward Hudec, it is a 24-floor building which combines modern style and decorative arts. With a height of 83.8 meters, it is the No. 1 Building of East Asia before 1983.

Pacific Hotel is an eclectic style building constructed in 1926. The most distinctive features are its ornate three-section facade, the gold-plated tower roof and the luxurious interior decoration.

Peace Hotel is one of the oldest buildings on Nanjing Road but still famous for its rooms of different styles such as Renaissance, Chinese, British, French, Spanish, German and Indian.

Pacific Hotel

Park Hotel, Pacific Hotel and Peace Hotel used to be the most luxurious hotels in old Shanghai and, being reminiscent of the past times, are still favorites of some nostalgic people.

By day Nanjing Road is a stream of people while at night it an ocean of lights. Lights of shopping malls, hotels and skyscrapers and neon signs constitute a most dazzling scene and the ever-bright Nanjing Road.

In recent years, East Nanjing Road has been developed into a walkway with parterres, sculptures, benches, sightseeing buses, and harmonious scenes.

Heaven of Cuisines   Nanjing Road offers a dazzling array of cuisines of different flavors. Some of the famous old restaurants are Meilongzhen, Green Willow Village Restaurant, Donghai Café, Xinya, Yangzhou Restaurant, Laozhengxing, Sichuang Restaurant, Yanyun Building, Zhujiang, Da San Yuan, etc. Of course there's no lack of stylish modern restaurants, for instance, the Olympics, Legendary Luminous Pearl and Paramount. Wufang Zhai, Shendacheng and Wangjiasha are well-known for their snacks like *xiefen xiaolong* (dumpling of crab meat), *longyan tianluo* (snail) and *sansi chunjuan* (spring roll).

Grand World   The Grand World is a most famous entertainment center in Shanghai that has gone through a history of more than 80 years.

It is a yellow building located at the intersection of East Yan'an Road and Xizang Road. Highlights include the hexagon gateway consisting of 12 pillars, the 55.3-meter-high spire, the extending overbridge

Paramount

Wangjiasha Snack Food Store

Nanjing Road Pedestrian Street

connecting all the buildings and the hypaethral square, which always presents performances.

Great World Entertainment Center

The Grand World was founded by a giant businessman named Huang Chujiu in 1917, and later, in 1930, it was run by Huang Jinrong, a gang leader. It opens everyday and presents performances like traditional operas, singing and dancing, folk art forms, acrobatics, magic, etc., which attract streams of visitors from all directions and make this pleasure ground well-known within the Far East.

Now the Grand World dedicates itself to developing entertaining categories with the traditional programs as the basis. It is the only agent of the Guinness World Records in China and on the No. 1 Arena, people can see unimaginable stunts. Recreational programs include Horror Palace, shooting the basket, toxophily and different kinds of electronic games; performances include traditional operas, acrobatics, magic, fashion show, etc.; "Old Shanghai" presents such programs as distorting mirror, rickshaw, teahouses and signboards, which could only be seen in the old days; and "Oriental Unique" shows traditional Chinese folk art forms like dough modeling, handicraft weaving, paper-cutting, etc.

Shanghai Art Museum Shanghai Art Museum is located at No. 456 West Nanjing Road. It is the cradle of China's fine arts in the modern times and boasts a collection ranging from modern oils and pop art to the Shanghai school of traditional Chinese art with Ren Bonian and Wu Changshuo as two representatives. Since 1956 when it's first opened, the museum has carried out 1,300 exhibitions of paintings, photographs and calligraphic works with over 300 coming from more than 40 different countries, including America, France, Canada, Britain, Italy, Demark, Switzerland, Spain, Japan, etc.

The art museum is a four-storied building topped with a towering belfry and occupying an area of 2,200 sq. m. Yellowy interior decoration reveals a quiet and peaceful atmosphere. Soft lights blaze the ways for visitors to art works. Shanghai Art Museum houses about 3,000 art works, including China's national treasures and foreign fine works.

Up to now it's the most modernized art museum in China and has advanced equipments of preservation, fireproofing and alarm system.

Shanghai Art Museum

Huaihai Road: The Champs Elysees Avenue of Shanghai

No road is as important as Huaihai Road in the heart of the Shanghai people. Having gone through a history of more than a century, Huaihai Road in Shanghai is a counterpart of the Champs Elysees Avenue in France, the Fifth Avenue in New York and Ginza in Tokyo.

Huaihai Road

Cathy Theatre

Names on the Move Constructed in 1901, Huaihai Road was originally named Baochang Road and later Xiafei Road and went through several others till it got to the present name. During the October Revolution, many Byelorussian refugees came to Shanghai and made a living by opening stores there. Xiafei Road in the French Concession turned into the oriental Neva Street and people of Shanghai called it Luosong Da Malu (Luosong Avenue) for "Russian" is pronounced "*luosong*" in Shanghai dialect. The road changed its name to Taishan Road during the Japanese invasion and after we achieved success in the War of Resistance against Japan, it was renamed to Linsen Road. In 1949, it was formally denominated as Huaihai Road to commemorate the great success of the Huaihai Battle and Shanghai's liberation.

Located in the previous French Concession, Huaihai Road boasts the sidewalks guarded by chinar trees on one side and European style architecture on the other side. In those days, many immigrants liked to live there and no city was like Shanghai to have immigrants from more than 50 different countries and regions. They took refugee in Shanghai and started their new life here by setting up different stores. As early as the 1920s and the 1930s, the 4-kilometre-long Huaihai Road has already become the "Fashion Fountainhead" in Shanghai. With European style arrangements and top brand collections released the same time with the Occident, the stores and restaurants here help Shanghai to keep its pace with the cities of developed countries. In the late 1920s, many such buildings as the Huaihai Fang, Shangfang Garden, Xinkang Garden and Wukang Building constructed one after another along Huaihai Road introduced Chinese elements into the road. Later some famous public architecture like the French Country Club also appeared and brought more scenes.

Shanghai International Shopping Center →

Verdant Greenness in High-rises

Today, Huaihai Road keeps its dignity and elegance though it's gone through many changes with the name. Time takes its past but never its charm and grace.

Middle Huaihai Road at Night

Fashion Foreland   The section from Shanxi Road to Xizang Road is the most booming part of Huaihai Road. More than several hundred department stores and speciality shops are located here, providing the pleasure of shopping and presenting beautiful concretionary music with the architecture.

Shanghai International Shopping Center makes good use of the space and creates the arrangement of "streets within the street, stores within the store, and gardens within the garden". Consisting of the shopping area, restaurants, entertainment center and offices and bureaux, it's overflowing with business atmosphere as well as cultural elegance. Printemps is another tasteful department store that aims to be the lead of international fashion and the art of life. It is a classical French style building framed harmoniously within the modern lines. The exterior with exquisite basso-relievo decoration always reminds people of the remote but beautiful Seine.

What brings out the best in each other with the commodities in the stores on Huaihai Road is the shopwindow dressing of different styles: European classicism, Chinese classicism, European fad, complicated mode, simple style, traditionalism and anti-conventionalism. The taste of Huaihai Road has kept upgrading and thus many famous brands came in succession to open their exclusive shops and chain stores here. Besides, counters are also set up in the department stores like Maison Mode, Lane Crawford and Iestan, where you can always find their new releases in the first time. Of course there are traditional Chinese department stores, for instance, the Shanghai Ladies Department Store, the Xue Bao Shopping Mall, the New Hualian Commercial Building and the Yimin Commercial Building.

Stores in Serried Ranks along Huaihai Road

Various Cuisines All along China boasts its food culture and a busy street like Huaihai Road is just a convergence of various cuisines. For Chinese cuisine, it has the Fulin Palace Seafood Restaurant, Datong Restaurant, Quan Ju De, Xian Yue Hien and Huaixiang Lou; while for Western food, no restaurant is more famous than the Red House, who sent their cooks to France to learn French cuisine and received many chiefs and leaders of different countries. Lao Da Chang, Chantilly and California Rainbow, are the most well-known bakery and café. Xiangdao Food Square and Guangming Cun sell tasty snacks of different flavors; and entertainment locations are just too numerous to mention one by one, such as Landai Entertainment Center, Night of Paris, Shanghai Garden Club and Times International.

Arched neon lights striding over Huaihai Road form a light tunnel every night, fascinating the people roaming there.

Red House

Shen Yue Xuan Restaurant

Literary Breeze The west section of Huaihai Road has always been the first choice for living and many celebrities' former residences are located here. In 1995, it welcomed a new member, that is, Shanghai Library on the intersection of Huaihai Road and Gao'an Road which boasts the OPAC system and the automatic transportation equipment. Occupying an area of more than 80,000 sq. m. with 3,000 seats and housing over 13,000,000 books, Shanghai Library is listed the No. 2 of China and among the Top Ten of the world. Artistic floor design, pillars in a circle and modern sculptures constitute the Knowledge Square in front of the library which creates a peaceful and literary atmosphere. The Wisdom Square at the corner of Gao'an Road embodies the concept of "the Wise Enjoys Water"with abstract sculptures and fountains.

After celebrating its 100th anniversary, Huaihai Road keeps changing with the world. Many high buildings sprouting out at the east section brought new energy to Huaihai Road and attracted top companies like Dupont, Compaq, Dow Jones, IBM, P&G, Bayer, Lucent, etc.

Shanghai Library

Confucius' Statue in Shanghai Library

Hengshan Road: Elegance Shaded by Phoenix Trees

If we compare roads to females, we can say Nanjing Road is like a modern girl, Huaihai Road a graceful lady and Hengshan Road a fairy gentlewoman. Quite and decent, Hengshan Road boasts fascination beyond compare.

Connecting with the prosperous Huaihai Road and extended by the commercial center Xujiahui, Hengshan Road is a beautiful and wide road guarded by phoenix trees on both sides with their shades covering

Hengshan Road

the sky and forming an extending corridor. One of the distinctive features of Hengshan Road is its sidewalks, which are decorated with flowering shrubs and give the passers-by the feeling of walking in an open park. With no grandness of Huaihai Road but, at the same time, no crowds of Nanjing Road, it boasts artistic architecture, elegant fences, distinctive shopwindows, broad roadway and sidewalks separated by iron barriers, benches and outdoor

Song Ziwen's Former Residence (today's Sasha's)

café, and classical Roman streetlamps illuminating the road and creating a soft and serene atmosphere.

The elegance of Hengshan Road has its origin. Previously named Beidang Road and located in the French Concession, it was the residential area of high officials, business tycoons and giants and foreigners. Like the houses on Hengshan Road are in the European style, people living here follow the lifestyle of the Occident and North America. No. 53 on Hengshan Road is the Christian Cathedral, a Gothic building with pointed arches, rib vaulting, flying buttresses covered by liana

Hengshan Hotel →

Kevin Café at the corner of Hengshan Road

Recreational Hengshan Road

and stone window frames and muntins. The Picasso Mansion (today's Hengshan Hotel) is a masterpiece of the Hungarian architect Ladislaus Edward Hudec. The Washington Mansion (today's Xihu Mansion) is another distinctive construction that helps to constitute the fascinating charm of Hengshan Road. With Western style buildings, engraved barriers and red tiles, it presents the scenes and features of Paris and composes a unique culture of Shanghai.

In recent years, Hengshan Road has been developed into a recreational and scenic street with many cafés, bars, teahouses, restaurants opened one after another. Decorated in widely different styles, they attract many young people and sweethearts to spend a leisure time in soft music and flickering candlelight.

Outdoor Café on Hengshan Road

Fenyang Road: Flowing Music and Poetry

Prosperity alone doesn't constitute a metropolis, which, beside the hurly-burly, needs serenity and sedateness. Thus, Shanghai still has several such delicate and peaceful roads as Sinan Road, Xinhua Road, Yuqing Road, Hu'nan Road, Xingguo Road, West Fuxing Road, Dongping Road, Shaoxing Road, Taiyuan Road, Yongjia Road, Taojiang Road, Kangping Road, Wukang Road, Tian'an Road and Fenyang Road that help to trigger the smile of the urbanites from the bottom of heart and make the unique city.

Stores at Shanghai Conservatory of Music

Here we pick Fenyang Road as particularization. Connecting with Huaihai Road and intersected by Yueyang Road, Fenyang Road is a beautiful phoenix-tree-shaded path that flows with music because the Shanghai Conservatory of Music is located here. Melodious music flows out of the school wall and inebriates the passers-by.

Buildings in Shanghai Conservatory of Music

Fenyang Road also boasts garden houses pleasing to both the eye and the mind. No. 45 is a Mediterranean style house with whitened walls, red tiles, artistic portico and carpet-like lawn. No. 79 is the Shanghai Arts and Crafts Research Institute, a French renaissance garden house reputed as "the Little White House".

The fishing touch of Fenyang Road is the bronze statue and monument of Alexander Pushkin, Father of Russian Literature and the famous poet who has a large amount of adorers all over the world. Every year on July 6, Pushkin's birthday, streams of adorers come from all directions to worship him with flowers and drape Fenyang Road with a poetic atmosphere.

Lofty phoenix trees block the hurly-burly and fickleness of the city and lock the flow of music and poetry, providing moments of ease for the busy urbanites.

Shanghai Arts and Crafts Research Institute

Pushkin's Statue

← Modern Architecture in Xujiahui

Xujiahui: Headspring of Vital Forces

Bordering the southwest area of Shanghai, Xujiahui is another commercial center with grand shopping malls and majestic buildings occupying an area of 120 hectares.

Former Xujiahui Road, Today's Zhaojiabang Road

Xu Guangqi's Statue →

Tomb of Xu Guangqi

Thriving Settlement of Celebrities According to the historical data, Xujiahui has been a key area as early as the Three Kingdoms period. Temples and joss houses were set up during the Wu Dynasty. Lady Huangdao Po, the outstanding weaving technology innovator of the Yuan Dynasty, resided in here and drove the textile industry. In the Ming Dynasty, the famous Chinese scientist Xu Guangqi (1562–1633) was born here. Actually Xujiahui (the Xu Family gathering) is named after him, a great contributor to the Chinese science and technology development and the first disseminator of Chinese and Western cultural and economic exchanges. Therefore, Xujiahui can be regarded as the cradleland of the cultural exchange of China and the Western countries.

Booming Shopping Malls Xujiahui aims to develop itself into a multi-functional, modernized and internationalized commercial area like Shinjuku and Tsim Sha Tsui.

Xujiahui has always been a thriving area with grand apartments and office buildings. The Xujiahui Square and Xujiahui Garden decorated with parterres and grasslands, together with many other architecture complexes, constitute a garden city zone of Xujiahui.

Orient Shopping Center is the first Shanghai-Hong Kong jointly owned commercial building that sells top-grade commodities in a comfortable shopping environment and also boasts entertainment center and restaurants.

Little Red Building

Hui Jin Department Store, a masterpiece of an American architect, is made up of 8 shopping floors and apartments of 28 stories. Grand Gateway is the principal construction of Xujiahui that occupies an area of 120,000 sq. m. and consists of hypermarkets, grand office buildings and majestic residential mansions. Metro City is the largest technological and multi-functional recreation center in Shanghai with cinema, KTV and MTV discotheque, Mini Disney World (No. 3 of Asia)

Thriving Xujiahui

and mini golf course. Other large-scale shopping malls in Xujiahui area include Pacific Department Store, Shanghai No. 6 Department Store and Hui Lian Department Store.

Fascinating Kaleidoscope Xujiahui is a kaleidoscopic area. St Ignatius Cathedral (1906) is the most important base of Catholicism in Shanghai. It is a Gothic church with a 70-meter-deep hall which can hold 2,500 Catholics, 64 columns with each consisting of 10 shafts with delicate carvings, and 31-meter-high pointed tower topped with a cross.

Shanghai Gymnasium located in Xujiahui area is the largest of Shanghai and has the well-equipped swimming pool. Nearby are the Longhua Temple, Tomb of Lady Huangdao Po and Shanghai Botanical Garden on the southeast; Xu Guangqi's Former Residence, Tomb of Xu Guanqi and Guangqi Park on Nandan Road; Guilin Park on the south; and the observatory with complete meteorological data. All these cultural treasures and modernized elements help Xujiahui keep being the headspring of vital forces.

Shanghai Stadium

Shanghai Weather Bureau

Duolun Road Cultural Street

Just off North Sichuan Road, the 550-meter-long Dunlun Road is a street lined with fine old houses, art supply stores, curio shops, galleries and teahouses. It's the cultural epitome of Shanghai and has witnessed Shanghai's development of 100 years. The area was once home to great writers like Lu Xun and so has been renamed the "Duolun Road of Famous Cultural Figures." Now it becomes a distinctive tourist attraction and the main appeal includes the Jinquan Coin Gallery, stone collection, chopsticks collection, Wang Zaoshi's fabulous collection of Mao badges, etc. Take a stroll through the street dotted with benches, statues, former residences and old houses, you are bound to find unique scenes.

Museum of Modern Art on Duolun Road

←Postman on Duolun Road Cultural Street

Old Building on Duolun Road

Old Movies Café on Duolun Road

City God Temple: Black Tiles and Red Columns

As an international metropolis, does Shanghai keep its style and features of the old days? In other words, where should we go if we want to have a look at the life that was on display in the streets of Shanghai in the old days? The answer is: the Old Town, the most traditional area of Shanghai and a fascinating place to wander. Yuyuan Garden and Bazaar located in the center of the Old Town is one of the well-preserved and Shanghai's premier sights. Though often overwhelmed with crowds, it is still well worth a visit.

City God Temple City God Temple is widely known in Shanghai as one of the main sightseeing highlights and visitors should give themselves at least half of the day to stroll around the area. Yuyuan Garden is the most famous classical garden in Shanghai and is harmoniously combined with the Zigzag Bridge, the Lotus Pond and the Mid-Lake Pavilion. The Chenxiangge Nunnery is a five-minute walk

Yuyuan Garden and Bazaar

City God Temple and the Zigzag Bridge

northwest of the Yuyuan Garden which is built in the Wanli Reign of the Ming Dynasty. The city's first mosque is situated on Fuyou Road. The City God Temple built in the Ming Dynasty has gone through a history of more than 600 years and 25 reconstructions. The last reconstruction can be traced back to 1927. It is a typical Chinese style building with a hall 4.8 *zhangs* (Chinese unit of length, 1 *zhang* = 3.3 meters) high, 4.1 *zhangs* wide and 6.3 *zhangs* deep, richly ornamented girders and ridgepoles, and jade green tiles and red eaves.

City God Temple

The Yuyuan Garden and Bazaar with the City God Temple as the center is the most distinctive place to see Shanghai folk custom and culture. Such folk arts shows as Lion Dance, Walking on Stilts, Boat Racing, Raising Bridal Sedan Chair, the Devil on two Sticks and Human Pyramid can always be seen on the squares there. Teahouses and restaurants present traditional string and woodwind music and sometimes *pingtan* (storytelling and ballad singing in Suzhou dialect). Stores along the streets sell handicrafts with living craft shows like paper-cut, moulding clay figurines, palm fiber weaving, sugar figurines blowing and pottery making. Some of them have become consummate skills. Elegance and grace also flow in the Old Town. Many archaized buildings hang steles or couplets, and the stores put up flag signboard of various shapes such as sword, shovel and triangle and different colors like apricot yellow, nacarat and dark black.

Antique Buildings in Yuyuan Garden and Bazaar

A New Lease of Life Though abundant in folk culture and humanistic scenery, the old City God Temple seemed narrow and crowded. After the reconstruction and expansion, it turns on a new look with the archaized building complex set up, including the Yuebin Lou (entertainment and shopping center), the Hefeng Lou (restaurant), the Tianyu Lou (department store), the Huabao Building (artworks store), the Jingrong Lou (jewelry store), the Jingyu Lou, the Jiushi Commercial Building, the Local Specialties Store, the Lakeside Restaurant and the Green Wave Gallery. With grand exterior decoration and delicate interior ornament, the most magnificent details should be the ancient stage and the balcony of the Huabao Building. The former boasts the woodworks carved with the lion head pattern and gilded sunk panels ornamented with jade-like stones; while the latter is a sumptuous masterpiece with carved lacquerware folding screen picturing the panorama of the Yuyuan Garden and Bazaar, twelve rosewood partition boards carved with the historical "Twelve Scenes of Shanghai", the gilded lamp holder with dragon patterns, and the white marble balustrades.

Fish View on the Zigzag Bridge

Shopping in Yuyuan Garden and Bazaar

A Complete Service of Shopping and Catering Stores of the Yuyuan Garden and Bazaar have always been famous for their distinctive features of smallness, specialty, high quality and completeness. Thousands of local specialties find favour in the customers' eyes. Some commodities without trace in big shopping malls can still be found here, such as pinheads, thread windings, wooden combs, round fans, folding fans, silk umbrellas and wooden chopsticks. Wandering around the City God Temple and finding small commodities is a pleasure for both the urbanites and tourists. The leisure and comfort reminds of the small stores in the old towns of Europe.

Besides distinctive small stores, here also offers a dazzling array of food and snacks. The Old Shanghai Restaurant, Green Wave Gallery, Lakeside Restaurant, Nanxiang Steamed Bun Restaurant, Songyun Building and Guihua Hall provide the visitors with an opportunity for cuisine exploration. Some of the restaurants such as the Green Wave Gallery have once received Queen Elizabeth II and Bill Clinton. And most of the dishes are ordinary meals of Shanghai and cost a quite reasonable price.

The night scene of the City God Temple is unique with eaves and ridges outlined by illuminations, rosewood palace lanterns and artistic lamps lightening the Mid-Lake Pavilion, and balconies contract pleasingly with the inverted reflections in water.

City God Temple at Night

Scarce Pure Land of the City

In a bustled metropolis like Shanghai, there are still several serene temples and monasteries that are leading a routine life and set up a unique scenic line of the city.

Longhua Temple

Longhua Temple   Southwest of central Shanghai, Longhua Temple occupies an area of 2.8 hectares and is the largest monastery in Shanghai. It is said to date from 242A.D. when the King of East Wu built it for his mother. The temple has been restored many times and the latest renovation is in 1875.

Longhua Temple is a complete architecture complex with five main halls: the Hall of Maitreya, the Hall of Heavenly God, the Precious Hall of the Great Hero, the Hall of the Three Saints and the Abbot Building. To either side of the entrance are a bell, a drum tower and the Hall of Arhats. With dark yellow walls and dark brown doors and windows, the temple looks magnificent and sacred.

Sculptures in Shanghai Martyrs Memorial

The Precious Hall of the Great Hero is a typical Chinese architecture with flying overlapped eaves, richly ornamented sunk panels pieced together with more than 4,000 arches. The Sakyamuni Statue is enshrined in the hall in a triad with the statue of Manjusri (the Bodhisattva

---

Longhua Pagoda

personifying supreme wisdom, depicted seated on a lion or on a lotus) and the statue of Samantabhadra (the Bodhisattva representing kindness or happiness, depicted seated on an elephant).

The adjoining Longhua Pagoda was originally built in 247 and has been reconstructed many times, most recently in 977. With flying eaves and winding balustrades, this 40.65-meter-high seven-story tower is the best preserved ancient pagoda in Shanghai.

West of the monastery used to be a peach garden which enjoyed great reputation for the peach blossoms in March and which now belongs to the next-door Shanghai Martyrs Memorial.

Longhua Temple has been carrying on some old customs such as the New Year Bell Strike and the temple fair. The famous 6,500 kg. bell in Longhua Temple is 2 meters high and used to be one of the eight scenes of Shanghai. Each year on the New Year's Eve, a stream of visitors come from all directions to listen respectfully to the 108 bell strikes and sermon. March 3 on the traditional Chinese lunar calendar is the time of the temple fair, which is to commemorate the death of Hop-pocket monk before he became Bodhisattva Maitreya. Wandering through the crowds and stands provides a good opportunity to acquaint yourself with the folk-custom of Shanghai.

A Panoramic View of Longhua Temple

Jade Buddha Temple   Located near the intersection of Anyuan Road and Jiangning Road, the Jade Buddha Temple is a distinctive architecture complex built in 1918 in the Song Dynasty style. The Heavenly King Hall, the Grand Hall and the Jade Buddha Building are in the center and the Reclining Buddha Hall, the Guan-yin Hall and the Abbot Room and the dining room are located on either side.

The story of the Jade Buddha Temple can be traced back to 1882, when Hui Gen, a monk from Putuo Mountain, traveled to Burma, lugged five jade Buddhas back to Putuo Mountain and left two of them in Shanghai: one seated Buddha and one reclining Buddha. A temple were built in Jiangwan Town for these two Buddhas but got destroyed in the war. Later, new site was chosen and the Jade Buddha Temple was set up to shelter them.

Buddha Statue in Jade Buddha Temple

The Grand Hall features three golden Buddhas: the Medicine Buddha, Sakymuni and Amithaba Buddha. The Jade Buddha Building features a 1-ton seated Buddha, which is 1.92 meters high and encrusted with jewels. It was carved with a complete Burmese jade and receives the appreciation from the visitors within and outside the country. The other treasure is the 96cm Buddha reclining on a mahogany couch. In 1989, another 4-meter-long reclining Buddha was given as a gift by the Singapore Buddhists. East of the temple is the Jade Buddha City, a peaceful and serene land with trees, flowers, waterfalls and streams.

Jade Buddha Temple

Jing'an Temple   No doubt the Jing'an Temple is the oldest monastery in Shanghai. It's said to be originally built in AD 247 during the Wu Dynasty of the Three Kingdoms period with the name Hudu Chongxuan Temple. In the Tang Dynasty, it was renamed Yongtai Monastery and didn't get the present name Jing'an Temple until 1008. Largely destroyed by the flood of Wusong River, the temple was moved to the intersection of today's Nanjing Road and Huashan Road. The temple has gone through several renovations and most of the present constructions are built after the Guangxu Reign of the Qing Dynasty. In 1880 (the sixth year during the Guanxu Reign of the Qing Dynasty), a Shanghai esquire named Li Chaojin and the official businessman Hu Xueyan provided the fund for the renovation of the gate of the temple and fenced the fountain at the gate, which is famed as "the No. 6 Fountain of the World" and alternatively named Boiling Well or Sea Eye.

The uniqueness of the Jing'an Temple might be its peace and sedateness contrasted clearly with the uproariousness of the busy Nanjing Road.

Jing'an Temple

Muen Christian Church Built in 1887 and located at the intersection of Middle Xizang Road and Jiujiang Road, this Christian church originally served as the ecclesia of the American supervisory board. It was named after a devotional Christian called Muen. A gothic church of red-brick was built in 1930, which has an auditorium that can contain more than 1,000 people and where holds religious ceremonies on Easter and Christmas every year. The East China Seminary is inside here.

Bible Casket

Mu'en Christian Church

International Community Church
Located at No. 53 Hengshan Road, International Community Church is built by emigrants from America and some other countries. It boasted the largest Christian church in Shanghai in 1925 when it's opened and can accommodate 700 people.

A Gothic red-brick building covered with vines, the L-shaped church consists of a main hall and a 3-storied podium building with the roof covered with ragstone tiles and the windows and altars featuring pointed arch decorations.

Interior of International Community Church

International Community Church

St Ignatius Cathedral St Ignatius Cathedral (1910) is a typical Gothic building of 56.6 meters high with one towering belfry on each side and fine stone carvings. It is known as the "No.1 Cathedral of the Far East."

Inside the cathedral there is a 44-meter-wide altar over which stands the statue of Virgin Mary. On the back wall there is a religious painting Last Supper. Decorated with colored glasses, the building looks grand and imposing. It can hold 3,000 people. In front of the cathedral there's a square of over 4,000 sq. m. and featuring a beautiful fountain.

St. Ignatius Cathedral

Sculpture of St. Ignatius Cathedral

Interior of St. Ignatius Cathedral

Chenxiangge Nunnery

Chenxiangge Nunnery No. 29 of Chenxiangge Road, this pleasant Bhiksuni complex is a key unit of cultural relics under the national protection. Originally named as Ciyun Buddhist Temple, Chengxiangge occupies an area of 2,378 sq. m. and the highlights include the Hall of Heavenly God, the Precious Hall of the Great Hero, the Kwan-yin Hall, etc.

City God Temple Built in 1403, the City God Temple is one of the major Taoist temples in Shanghai. Statues of city gods Qin Yubo and Huo Guang are offered sacrifice in the temple, which received endless streams of pilgrims in the Qing Dynasty.

City God Temple

Life·Shanghai

If Xi'an features its history, Beijing features its politics and Guangzhou features its entertainment, Shanghai features its life. For almsost 100 years, Shanghai has always leading the fashions, either in basic necessities of life or entertainment items. Mixing and matching highlights from all corners of the earth, Shanghai forms its own style. With a booming economy, it's a Happy Land to live.

Restaurants: Heaven of Cuisines

China has long been famous for the distinctive Chinese culinary art and enjoys a worldwide reputation as the "kingdom of cuisine". And it's no exaggeration we say Shanghai, as a cosmopolitan city, is a heaven of cuisines. Not only all the eight regional cuisines of China can be found in Shanghai, but Shanghai offers a dazzling display of new delicacies as well. Besides, the restaurants with distinctive design and original decoration provide a nice environment and upgrade the culinary art from eating for survival to eating for enjoyment.

But how can we make the best choices for good taste, nice environment and distinctive originality from thousands of restaurants in Shanghai? Let's draft a map by connecting all the delicious localities.

Noble House

Building 1 of An Ting Villa Hotel, No. 46 Anting Road
Tel: 64333666
Average expense: 300 RMB/person

Atmosphere: A Spanish style house built in 1934, Noble House used to be a hotel which once received Khrushchev and Ho Chi Minh. Great changes time brought to the world didn't deprive it of the charm and elegance. With more illuminations installed and antique things like the garden, the fireplace,

Noble House

the engraved glass windows and the timepiece made by Johnson Bros kept untouched as before, it is the best place to remember past times.

Special delicacies recommendation: Classical Guangdong Cuisine, original Cantonese food like abalone and shark fin, shark fin with crab, tofu with crab, asparagus with crab, scalded daylily, and steamed crab from Yangcheng Lake.

Kong's Garden

Kong's Garden

> No. 336 South Wanping Road
> Tel: 64683159
> Average expense: 50–70 RMB/person

Atmosphere: Kong Xiangxi's Former Residence, this is a 80-year-old villa restaurant. It boasts the antique atmosphere with a red pavilion, the 120-year-old stone pine, walls laid with grey bricks and a cluster of red lanterns.

Special delicacies recommendation: Mainly Shanghai cuisine such as fish stuffed with mutton, Mandarin fish on bamboo web, club beef steak with black pepper, shrimps with potherb, trotter cooked with lotus leaf, mushroom with consommé of abalone, crisp shrimp and eel in bamboo tube.

Nanling Restaurant

Nanling Restaurant

> No. 168 Yueyang Road
> Tel: 64677381
> Average expense: 100–120 RMB/person

Atmosphere: Simple Western style decoration with a quiet and cozy garden.

Special delicacies recommendation: Yangzhou cuisine with the chef being the granddaughter of Mo Youcai, a Yangzhou cook

renowned in the South, and the restaurant reputed as Mo's Kitchen. Two musts are Slices of Dried Bean Curd with Crab and lionshead meatballs with crab.

Yuan Yuan Restaurant

No. 201 Xingguo Road

Tel: 64339123

Average expense: 60-80 RMB/ person

Atmosphere: simple and elegant decoration and pleasing and cozy environment.

Special delicacies recommendation: Shanghai's indigenous cuisine famous for braised pork, fried pomfret fish, corn with salt and pepper, spare ribs in brown sauce and jujube with glutinous rice.

Old Shanghai Station

No. 201 North Caoxi Road

Tel: 64272233

Average expense: 100–150 RMB/person

Atmosphere: Exquisite and antique, the restaurant used to be a famous monastery. With floor-length windows, mottled wooden floor, old pictures, an antiquated typewriter and an archaic gramophone, it's more like an antique library. The most distinctive feature is the old carriages and the locomotive parked in the garden, and they serve as dining-rooms. The carriages have a long history. The one made in Germany in 1899 was part of the private train of Queen Cixi and the other made in Russia in 1919 came from the special train for Song Qingling.

Special delicacies recommendation: smoked fish, beef slices, crystalline shrimps, etc.

Old Shanghai Station

Sophie's Tea & Restaurant

No. 99 Middle Huaihai Road, 4th floor of Times Square

Tel: 63910152

Average expense: 130–180 RMB/person

Atmosphere: Commodious and delicate restaurant with living violin and piano shows.

Special delicacies recommendation: steamed slices of dried bean curd, eggplant pie, honey ham and dry fried cod fish with noodles.

Old Shanghai Restaurant

No. 133 Hongqiao Road (Hongji Square)
Tel: 64077572
Average expense: 60 RMB/person

Atmosphere: A Shikumen-style building decorated with grey bricks, black-painted gate, arched basso-relievo details and original names of the traditional Shanghai lanes like Anfu Li, Bugao Li and Yongyu Li.

Special delicacies recommendation: Shanghai's indigenous cuisine with crab and shrimp as its special delicacies.

Cu Cai Guan

No. 1697 Xinzha Road
Tel: 62553633
Average expense: 60–80 RMB/person

Atmosphere: Under the signboard of movie stars, the restaurant boasts Hong Kong movie stars and one of the owners named Cai Lan, a famous gourmet from Hong Kong.

Old Shanghai Restaurant

Special delicacies recommendation: typical Cantonese cuisine such as pheasant rolls with laver, carbon roasts pork, rice with lards oil and ice and fire fish.

Jintuodao Restaurant

No. 24 Second East Zhongshan Road
Tel: 63281666
Average expense: 80–100RMB/person

Atmosphere: A rooftop restaurant with beautiful views of the architecture on the Bund and Jinmao Tower and the Oriental Pearl TV Tower in Pudong.

Special delicacies recommendation: original Chaozhou food such as fish stewed with brown sauce, baked spats, geese feet pot with mushroom and crisp roast pork.

Windmill Restaurant

No. 1440 Hongqiao Road
Tel: 62197514
Average expense: 100 RMB/person

Impression

Atmosphere: A green-shaded villa restaurant with teak tables, antique pendant lamps, old pictures of movie stars and reminiscent melodies.

Special delicacies recommendation: quick-fried shrimps and stewed sliced fish in wine sauce.

Impression
No. 145 South Shanxi Road
Tel: 64725719
Average expense: 50–70 RMB/person

Atmosphere: Antique and typical Chinese-style with elegant decoration and exquisite dishware.

Special delicacies recommendation: Creative Shanghai cuisine like korean style roasted pork chop, orange bowl, fruit flavor shrimp ball and rice in straw bag (the idea comes from the countryside of Fujian Province, where the farmers take rice in straw bags when they go working in mountains and heat them up before eating).

Zen Cantonese Cuisine Restaurant

House 2 South Block, Xintiandi, Lane 123, Xingye Road
Tel: 63856382
Average expense: 100–120 RMB/person

Atmosphere: A work of British interior designer Andre Fu who pays much attention to decoration details and cultural connotation, reputed as one of the Top Ten Chinese Restaurants by the media abroad.

Special delicacies recommendation: chicken wings in glutinous rice, mushroom with consommé of abalone and Shi Dan (a dish with egg underlayer, middle layer of shrimp and roast geese and dried scallop on the top, Cantonese homophonic with Mandarin "suibian" (whatever), and best-choice when you do not know what to order).

Hongyun Lou

No. 567 Zhaojiabang Road

Tel: 64435305

Average expense: 60~80 RMB/person

Atmosphere: A Chinese style restaurant with archaized entrance, engraved lattice windows and celadon vases.

Special delicacies recommendation: drunken green crabs, fried suckling pigeon and Hongyun hotchpotch.

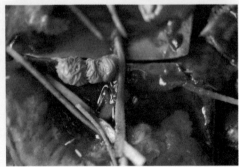

Hongyun Lou

Ba Guo Bu Yi

Ba Guo Bu Yi

No. 1676 Hongqiao Road

Tel: 62706668

Average expense: 50–70 RMB/person

Atmosphere: A Sichuan style teahouse-like restaurant with living Sichuan opera.

Special delicacies recommendation: crisp intestine fried on stones, crucian with bean curd and spicy fish.

Dongbeiren Restaurant

No. 1 South Shanxi Road

Tel: 52288288

Average expense: 50–70 RMB/person

Atmosphere: Rice-storehouse-style decoration with clusters of broomcorn and corn, hospitable waiters and waitresses in bright green and red and living shows of errenzhuan, a song-and-dance duet in the Northeast of China.

Special delicacies recommendation: Braised Chicken with Mushroom, Braised Eggplant with Potato, Chops with Soy Sauce, Straw-hat Cake and Corn Drinks.

Old Xianheng Hotel Restaurant

> No. 139 East Yincheng Road
> Tel:58827979
> Average expense: 60–80 RMB/person

Atmosphere: Simple, antique, elegant and quiet with a try square counter facing the entrance, two celadon wine jugs with red-cloth lids placed on one end of the counter, bamboo chopsticks containers and blue-rimmed bowls.

Special delicacies recommendation: Creative Shaoxing cuisine such as beans flavored with aniseed, shrimp in wine sauce, Shaoxing flavor lobster, salted fish and dumplings coated with sesame.

Qianxiang Ge

> Near intersection of Pucheng Road and Shangcheng Road in Pudong
> Tel: 58871717
> Average expense: 50–60 RMB/person

Atmosphere: Combination of wildness and modernness with walls laid with grey bricks, two water screens and stone mortars working as the washbasins of the toilets.

Special delicacies recommendation: chicken with chilli and fish soup with pickled Chinese cabbage.

Duo Shuai Gong

> No. 18 Gaolan Road (near Sinan Road)
> Tel: 53069151
> Average expense: 50 RMB/person

Atmosphere: Li Hongzhang's Former Residence, a Beijing style decoration with palace lanterns and old pictures.

Special delicacies recommendation: authentic Beijing cuisine such as roast duck, instant-boiled mutton from Xinjiang, Beijing distilled spirit and sesame seed cakes.

Kong Yiji's Statue

Snacks: Make Taste Bud in Full Bloom

Snacks have always been a non-replaceable part in Chinese cuisines. Simple but delicious, Chinese snacks are postprandial refreshments and sometimes can serve as dinner. Without any rules of restaurant etiquette, snacks are one of the best ways to know the daily life of Chinese people and culture.

Yunnan Road Food Street

The good luck of living in Shanghai is that, like the city itself, the snacks here are also very cosmopolitan, that is, there are multifarious snacks. Some of the famous places are the City God Temple area, Wujiang Road, Yunnan Road, etc.

Wujiang Road Food Street

Steamed Meat Dumplings →

Fuchun Steamed Meat Dumpling Store
No. 650 Yuyuan Road
Tel: 62525117

Famous for Yangzhou snacks, this store boasts the steamed meat dumplings, which, after five procedures, is tasty but not greasy. Sago syrup and mashed jujube cake are two best-sell desserts.

Fried Dumplings →

Wenzhou Wonton
No. 67 Second Ruijin Road
Tel: 53061817

Rice-Flour Noodles

Wonton is the favorite snack of many Chinese people and this store boasts dimetric and oblate wontons. Thin skin, fresh stuffing, pure color and consommé soup with egg slices, shrimp, laver, two quail eggs and fish balls constitute a bowl of delicious wonton. Sometimes they are served with tapped fish soup, which is made by tapping fish and flour into a cake, cutting the cake into slices and cooking with egg slices, slices of preserved szechuan pickle, mushroom slices and water. It was once listed as one dish of the state banquet.

Laoma Rice-Flour Noodles

Laoma Rice-Flour Noodles
No. 2118 North Sichuan Road
Tel: 56712335

With material from Yunnan and flavor of Sichuan, Laoma Rice-Flour Noodles boasts rice-flour noodles braised with mushroom and chicken. Another delicacy is fried dumplings on iron plate with leek and egg as the stuffing and the iron plate as the heat preservation.

Jia's Steamed Stuffed Bun

No. 638 South Henan Road

Tel: 63663570

You can always find people queuing here for steamed stuffed buns. One specialty is "first-order-then-cook". They make buns only on orders from the customers and boasts the variety of the stuffing such as pork meat, crab meat and mixed meat.

White Soup Noodles

No. 380 Tianyaoqiao Road

Tel: 642777542

People from Dongtai, Jiangsu Province always start their day with a bowl of white soup noodles. The soul of the noodle is its soup which is made of fresh crucian fish, ribs and eel bones. White soup noodles in Dongtai has no dipa while Shanghai people like to put some pickles and meat slices. You can also pay 2 yuan for a bowl of soup which takes 3 to 4 hours to cook.

Ahniang Noodles Store

No. 19 Sinan Road

Tel: 53066604

Ahniang Noodles

Ahniang is what people from Ningbo of Zhejiang Province call their

Fried Steamed Bread

grandmother. To commemorate the owner of the store, an old lady from Ningbo, people replace its original name "Taihe Refreshment House" with Ahniang Noodle Store. In one gastronomic book introducing where to eat in Shanghai, Ahniang noodles were regarded as the most delicious noodles. Yellow croaker noodles are the most-known here and shrimp noodles and crab noodles also sell well.

Yuanyuanxiang Wonton
No. 360 Guangdong Road
Tel: 63201298

A Taiwan style snack store, it boasts the small and conglobate wonton, fried spring rolls, fried bean curd and dumplings.

With countless delicious snacks but a small budget, you should go to snack food streets such as Wujiang Road and Yun'nan Road and City God Temple area, which run business until early morning and boast good and cheap snacks like vermicelli soup with fried bean curd puff, chicken or duck blood soup, glutinous rice dumplings, red bean soup with sweet-scented osmanthus, sweet lotus seed porridge, wine dumplings, pumpkin pies, Sinkiang kabob, Chang'an dumplings, roast sweet potato, tofu with chopped deep-fried twisted dough sticks, fried gluten puff soup with soya milk film and fried stuffed cakes. With 10 to 20 yuan, you can definitely eat your fill.

Bars: Shelter of Urban Souls

With the spirit of aestheticism and cynicism, bars in Shanghai are like espressos which tell the romance, the pathos, the warmth, the sweetness, the bitterness and the sadness of the city.

Hengshan Road and South Maoming Road are two well-known bar streets in Shanghai. In many people's eyes, they are the mark of places to relax their rundown souls. Like an open bar itself, Hengshan Road is distinctive for its bold and unrestrained style. South Maoming Road, however, seems not that roaring much relaxing with low doors, flickering candlelight, soft music and gorgeous lights.

An indispensable color of Shanghai, bars complete the romance and beauty of the city's nights.

Jazz Bar of Peace Hotel

> No. 20 East Nanjing Road, 1st floor of Peace Hotel
> Atmosphere: reminiscent
> Average Expense: 120 RMB/person
> Main Customers: nostalgic people

Jazz Bar of Peace Hotel kept being the first bar in Shanghai for twenty years and was definitely the symbolization of social status in those days. It even became the symbolization of the nation's culture because listening to Jazz at the bar was one program when foreign state chiefs came to visit

Jazz Bar of Peace Hotel

Shanghai. Margaret Thatcher, Ronald Reagan and Francois Mitterrand have all been here and now the bar still boasts the majestic and elegant decoration and the Old Jazz Band.

Cloud Nine

No. 88 Century Avenue of Pudong New Area, 88th floor of Hyatt Hotel

Atmosphere: post-modern style

Average expense: 80 RMB/person

Main Customers: white collars

With a height of 320 meters, this is one of the highest bars in the world. The stainless steel frame gives the feeling of chilliness but the beautiful scene of the night Shanghai and various colorful cocktails warm the heart of everyone there.

Cloud Nine of Hyatt Hotel

FACE

No. 118 Second Ruijin Road, Building 4 of Ruijin Hotel

Atmosphere: post-modern style

Average Expense: 50–60 RMB/person

Main Customers: foreigners, artists and fashionable youngsters

Face

Face

A 19th century French-style house shaded in bushy phoenix trees, FACE boasts the old fashioned square table and the antique opium bed on which customers can lie, smoke, drink or sip tea. In flickering lights, ladies in cheongsams or Western-style dresses present glamorous nights of Shanghai.

Qiong Ren Jian

No. 150 Yueyang Road

Atmosphere: yuppie

Qiong Ren Jian

Average Expense: 60 RMB/ person

Main Customers: young people

Different from the bars on landmark-like Hengshan Road and the classical Maoming Road, Qiong Ren Jian uniquely introduces the concept of Chinese gardens into its decoration and is shaded with bamboos. Each seat is illuminated by two lights from above, enlightening the table and cups but leaving the customers in hazy shadows.

The Door

The Door

No. 1460 Hongqiao Road
Atmosphere: classical
Average Expense: 80 RMB/person
Main Customers: cultured people and
white collars

As the name tells, the bar consists of scores of doors with each telling a story. An epitome of China's history and culture, the doors vary from engraved wooden plates of the Tang Dynasty to arched garden gates of the Ming and Qing Dynasties. Set off by the multifarious laser lights and lintels of antique or modern styles, they build up a unique humanistic scene in Shanghai.

Marco Polo

No. 200 Xinhua Road
Atmosphere: reminiscent
Average Expense: 20 RMB/person
Main Customers: cultured people

A work of Mr. Deng Kunyan, the famous Taiwan designer, the bar is a classical humanistic piece: a cracky crosstie working as the bar counter, old pictures of movie and sport stars recalling the past, antique gramophone playing nostalgic songs and two paper lamps giving off dim light.

Marco Polo

Ritz

No. 1376 West Nanjing Road, 2nd floor of Portman Ritz-Carlton Hotel
Shanghai
Atmosphere: jazz
Average Expense: 60 RMB/person
Main Customers: senior white collars

Located on the corridor of the Portman Ritz-Carlton Hotel Shanghai, it has the first-class jazz band that conveys a brand-new concept of classical and modern jazz. When Bill Clinton came to visit Shanghai, he lived in this hotel and played saxophone at the bar, which is now shown during the intervals of the band.

Cigar Bar

No. 728 Pudong Avenue , 4th floor of Novotel Atlantis Hotel Shanghai
Atmosphere: fashionable
Average Expense: 30–50 RMB/person
Main Customers: cigar smokers

With cigar smell very much in the air, even non-smokers can't help drawing a deep breath every so often. The bar sells hundreds of cigars (mainly Cuban cigars) and cigar kits and build up a heroical atmosphere which reminds people of Winston Churchill, Che Guevara and Fidel Castro.

La Seine

No. 236 First East Zhongshan Road
Atmosphere: humanistic
Average Expense: 40 RMB/person
Main Customers: cultured people, artists and lovers of Paris culture

The left bank of La Seine has always been regarded as the symbolization of Paris' culture and this bar is quite of its style. With antique and exquisite fresco pieces and pendant lamps of the Bourbon Dynasty, it recalls the history and brilliant culture of that time.

Cigar Bar

Shu Xiang Men Di

No. 699 Xinhua Road
Atmosphere: yuppie
Average Expense: 60 RMB/person
Main Customers: literature lovers

With shelves of hardcover original editions and all waitresses being university students who major in art and can talk about history, philosophy and literature, the bar attracts a stream of customers and even some scholars.

Han Yuan

Old China Hand Resources Reading Room (Han Yuan)
No. 27 Shaoxing Road
Atmosphere: humanistic
Average Expense: 60 RMB/person
Main Customers: cultured people

Located on a phoenix-tree-shaded street, it's a bar as well as a bookstore. With casebound books, a romantic and quiet environment, Western and Chinese antiques such as the ancient lighter, typewriter, camera and age-old steles of the Ming and Qing Dynasties displayed and classical Western music flowing within the room, this is a must place for all the foreigners in Shanghai.

South Maoming Road, a Bar Street

Excursions: Pondering over the Details of the City

Shanghai boasts many places worth visiting and there are plenty of day and overnight trips to be made inside and outside Shanghai. They either attract visitors with the lingering charm of traditional Chinese culture or surprise them with annotations of modern fashion and art. Delicate details of Shanghai, these places, like the symbolic buildings, also reflect the cultural spirit and essence of the city.

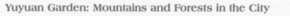

Yuyuan Garden: Mountains and Forests in the City

Yuyuan Garden, located in the northeast of the Old Town area of Shanghai, is a famous classical garden and reputed as "the most amazing garden of the South", "crown garden in Southeast China", and "mountains and forests in the city" with whitened walls, black tiles and archaic pavilions, terraces, booths and buildings.

Yuyuan Garden

Yuyuan Garden has gone through a history that dates from more than 400 years ago. The owner of the garden, Pan Yunduan, once a treasurer of Sichuan Province, had the garden built to please his father in his old age. Hence the name of the garden "Yu", which means "pleasing one's parents". Occupying an area of over 70 *mus* (Chinese unit of area, 1 *mu* = 1/15 of a hectare), it is a masterpiece of Zhang Nanyang, a famous landscape architect of the Ming Dynasty, and reflects the artistic style of the Ming and Qing Dynasties.

Sansui Hall of Yuyuan Garden

Today Yuyuan Garden is divided into five scenic sections by five dragon walls, excluding the Mid-lake Pavilion, the Zigzag Bridge and the Lotus Pond.

Yangshan Hall and Rockery Hill   Entering the garden, you will see the Three Corn-Ear Hall, a complete wooden construction with three plaques hanging inside—"Mountain and Forests in the City" on top, "Ling Tai Jin Shi" in the middle and "Three Corn-Ear Hall" at the bottom. The name "Three Corn-Ear Hall" reflects the wishes for a rich harvest, and for the same reason, there are crops, corns and fruits carved on the doors of the hall. Behind the Three Corn-Ear Hall stands the Yangshan Hall (Hall for Viewing the Mountain), opposite which is a beautiful rockery hill. This 14-meter high rockery hill is dumped with 2,000 tons of rocks from 200-kilometer-away Wukang

Rockery Hill in Yuyuan Garden

in Zhejiang Province and noted for its steep cliffs and hidden, winding paths. It is the only preserved artwork of Zhang Nanyang and a rarity in Southern China. Mr. Chen Congzhou, a famous contemporary expert of ancient classical gardens and architecture, once highly praised the rockery hill by saying "with the rockery covered by trees and flowers and the streams flowing down the slopes into the pond below, I enjoy so much the scenery here on this mountain ridge". On the hilltop there is a pavilion which commands an excellent view of the Huangpu River. Above the Yangshan Hall is the "Rain Rolling Tower" and behind is the Cuixiu Hall where display ten red sandalwood fans carved with the verses of famous poets of China.

Chamber of Ten Thousand Flowers

Happy Fish Waterside Pavilion and Chamber of Ten Thousand Flowers　East of the Yangshan Hall is a corridor and at the entrance to the corridor are two iron lions cast in the Yuan Dynasty. The Taihu rock not far away from the corridor looks like a young lady and is thus named "Beauty's Waist". Passing the moon-shaped door, you will see the Happy Fish Waterside Pavilion, a good place for enjoying goldfish swimming happily in the pond. Beside the pavilion is the Double Corridor partitioned by a wall with latticed windows. Looking through the windows, you will see beautiful views of streams and rocks on your right and chambers and towers on your left. On the left side of the Double Corridor is the Chamber

Happy Fish Waterside Pavilion

of Ten Thousand Flowers surrounded by winding cloisters. It is so called because it was the historical site of the Flower Goddess Pavilion of the Ming Dynasty and there are fresh flowers here all the year round.

Spring Hall and the Hall of Mildness Spring Hall, a grand and majestic building in Yuyuan Garden, once served as the headquarters of the northern city command of the Small Sword Society, a secret organization during the Taiping Revolution. Opposite the hall is a stone stage built in the Qing Dynasty, which looks like a pavilion on the water and which is decorated with carvings and gilded paintings. Northwest of the pavilion is an ancient well pavilion, and there is a octagonal well in the middle of the pavilion. The Hall of Mildness faces the Spring Hall across a pond. All the practical and beautiful furniture here is made of banian tree roots. The plum tree in front of the hall is more than 150 years old and reputed as the "Plum Tree King".

Spring Hall

The Hall of Mildness

Scenery Gathering Tower and Exquisite Jade Stone The Scenery Gathering Tower is the center of one of the three scenic sections in the eastern part of Yuyuan Garden and commands an excellent view of the whole garden. Surrounded by water on three sides, it boasts various trees such as camphor trees, megranate trees, maple trees, jacaranda trees and podocarp trees, the 2-meter-high rose sandalwood folding screen enchased with jade, agate, emerald and dragon pattern, as well as the exquisite dragon tables and chairs all dating back to the Qing Dynasty. East of the tower is a one-hundred-meter-long water corridor, the longest of its kind in Southern China. Next to the corridor is a three-zigzag bridge and

on the end of the bridge is a wall with a moon-shaped door. The words "*Yinyu*" (leading to the jade) are above the door. Passing the door, you will enter the next scenic section: the Exquisite Jade Stone. The Exquisite Jade Stone is a rare treasure of Southern China and one of the three best Taihu stones in China (the other two are in Suzhou and Hangzhou respectively). The stone is noted for its slender shape, translucent nature, wrinkled surface and numerous holes. Smoke from incense sticks burned below coils up through the holes, while water poured on the top drips down through them.

Hall of Serenity and Guantao Building The Inner Garden is a small but delicate garden within Yuyuan Garden. The Hall of Serenity, a major

Scenery Gathering Tower

← Exquisite Jade Stone

Ancient Theatrical Stage

structure in the Inner Garden, is a wide and deep building with age-old trees and a beautiful pond. West of the hall is the Guantao Building (Building for Viewing the Billows), a three-story wooden structure. It is so named because it's the highest architecture in the Qing Dynasty and commands an excellent view of the rivers and billows on the far distance. The ancient theatrical stage is once reputed as "the No. 1 Stage of the Gardens in Southern China" with carved girders, painted ridgepoles, gilded woodcarvings and a magnificent dome-like caisson ceiling which is made up of 22 circles, 20 arcs and 28 flying golden birds and acquires good sound effects. The Ancient Theatrical Stage can contain an audience of 300 people and provides VIP seats right opposite the stage.

Five essential scenic spots of the classical Yuyuan Garden are: the Rockery Hill, the Exquisite Jade Stone, the five dragon walls, the bricking carvings and clay sculptures and the Inner Garden.

Dragon Wall of Yuyuan Garden

Xintiandi: New Fashion of Old Longtang

It is said that *Shikumen* houses and old *Longtang* (alleys) are one of the best choices if you want to know the life of Shanghai. Xintiandi, this ambitious new business, entertainment and cultural complex, now draws a full stop to them. It consists of several blocks of renovated traditional *shikumen* houses and occupies an area of 30,000 sq. m. With many cafés, restaurants, boutiques, speciality shops, galleries and bars, many people, especially tourists first coming to Shanghai, will feel lost. But this contributes to its distinctive feature, that is, arousing the visitors' curiosity for ever.

Xintiandi, a Shikumen Architecture Complex

The complex, with original brick walls, tiles and black doors but modern interior decorations, reminds people of the life of the 1920s and, at the

Xintiandi at Night

same time, presents the most fashionable elements.

Being public and openness are two distinctive features of Xintiandi complex, which differ it from any other alleys in Shanghai. The whole complex is flooded with excellent combinations of Western and Chinese elements: foreigners come to see Shanghai-style culture and Chinese come to enjoy Western atmosphere. This kind of combination bringing bang up to date with a stylish modern twist makes Xintiandi one best gathering spot for cultured people and many foreigners.

Xintiandi is also a place where you can easily communicate with movie stars such as Jackie Chan and many celebrities because many restaurants in Xintiandi are owned by them. The TMSK Xintiandi Restaurant owned by Yang Huishan, a famous Taiwan actress, inspires you when wining and dining in a colored glass palace; singing and dancing performances of

Xintiandi—Shanghai's Recreation Center

French-style restaurants and cellar restaurants bring the romance of France; Live House Xintiandi ARK plays rock-and-roll combining tradition with modernness and reminiscence with fashion; and Brazilian barbecue takes you to the far South America.

This is Xintiandi, a stylish traditional and modern complex imbued with the city's historical and cultural legacies and comprising specialist food and beverage, retail, entertainment, conference and exhibition as well as tourism facilities.

Site of the 1st National Congress of the CCP

Site of the 1st National Congress of the CCP

During the more than one hundred years' history after the Opium War, many patriots struggled with utmost fortitude for the liberation, independence and prosperity of the Chinese nation.

No, 76 Xingye Road is a two-story Shikumen style building that hosted the 1st National Congress of the Chinese Communist Party (CCP) on July 23, 1921. Three halls exhibit more than 200 precious historical materials.

Simulation of the 1st National Congress of the CCP

Liuhe Road and Dongtai Road: Heaven of Antiquers

In Beijing, all antiquers know the age-old colored glaze factory, while in Shanghai, curio lovers always go to the Liuhe Road and the Dongtai Road, which are full of lines of stores and famous for grotesquerie, rarity, specialty and oddness. You can find almost anything here: classical furniture of the Ming and Qing Dynasties, jade articles, porcelain, bronze ware, bamboo articles, tinwork, paintings and calligraphy and daily necessities of Shanghai people in the 1920s to the 1930s such as medieval phonographs,

Dongtai Road and Liuhe Raod

kerosene lampshade, almanacs, cigarette packages, lighters, shavers, cricket fighting kits, electric fans, etc. Most of the customers here are able to tell good from bad and, if one gets on well with the owner of a store, he or she will be treated as a bosom friend and shown all the collections by the store owner. Wandering about various antiques and curios, people recall the past and cherish more the present. Besides the antiquers, these two streets attract many visitors from home and abroad.

Taikang Road: Habitat of Art Lovers

Having been quiet and unknown to the public for many years, Taikang Road, a path located in Luwan District of Shanghai, suddenly became famous because many Chinese and foreign artists set their studios here. A distinctive feature and relative advantage of Taikang Road is its geographical position and historical and cultural connotation: it is next to Shaoxing Road, the famous "publishing street" in Shanghai, and the architectures here are excellent combinations of Chinese and Western elements at all times. Since 1997, artists such as Chen Yifei and Er Dongqiang have successively set their studios on Taikang Road.

Later, many top companies, cultural brokers and law offices chose Taikang Road to settle and more than ten foreign artists set up their design studios and workrooms. Now there are 105 business stands on Taikang Road, occupying a business area of 10,000 sq. m. An Art Street is gradually coming into being.

Studios at Taikang Road

5

Vernal sea breeze, undulant roads, waist-high weeds, birds' nests deep in swamps, streams and waters extending into the distance, happily swimming fishes and jumping shrimps, crisscross footpaths between fields, verdant cornfields and golden ears, bamboo-guarded narrow lanes and winding stone paths, streams joining flagstone streets and arced stone bridge viewing soundlessly the setting sun... Many people would be greatly surprised if they were told that all these can be seen in Shanghai. As a matter of fact, besides the high buildings and heavy traffic, Shanghai also has rural scenes and countrified beauty. Urbanites are just too busy to notice. A metropolis without rurality is like Paris without Fontainebleau or Vienna without forest. Like gigantic lungs or kidneys, countrified scenes are indispensable adjustors of the city that help bring a healthier and longer life.

Songjiang: Xanadu of Emperor Shoumeng of Wu State

Songjiang was the oldest town of Shanghai and more than 2,000 years ago, when Shanghai was still beneath the sea, it was thriving already. In 751, Songjiang has already developed itself into an important town in Southeast China. Now Songjiang boasts its centuries-old but brilliant history and culture and has the most ancient architecture and cultural relics of Shanghai.

Catholic Sheshan Cathedral

Sheshan National Forest Park Sheshan is the only part of Shanghai to have mountains and forests. Actually there are more than 20 mountains extending continuously 13 kilometers. In Chinese, the number "9" is no more than ten and thus auspicious, so people call these mountains as "nine peaks". The area is named Sheshan (She Mountain) because She Mountain is the most famous of all. Standing in the Scenery View Tower on east She Mountain, you will be greeted by a scroll of countrified paintings.

The Jesuit Observatory is the first one in Shanghai and set up by French missionaries in 1899.

The Catholic Sheshan Cathedral was built in 1871, expanded in 1925 and is reputed as "the No. 1 Cathedral in the Far East". A baroque-style building, it also adopts Grecian, Roman, Gothic

No. 1 Building of Songjiang District

Sheshan Mountain

and Chinese elements. Magnificently perched on top of the hill, it can be easily seen from far.

Leaning Tower on Heaven Horse Mountain

Leaning Tower on Heaven Horse Mountain   Heaven Horse Mountain (Tianmashan) is the highest peak of all the mountains and is thus named because it looks like a heaven horse. On the mountain there is a Huzhu Pagoda built in the Northern Song Dynasty and known as the leaning tower of China. The 7-story tower started tilting 200 years ago and now has an inclination of 6° 51' 52" , exceeding the tower at Pisa. Though having gone through many violent storms, the tower still stands and attracts a stream of visitors.

Pool of Drunken Bai   On Renming Road of Songjiang District there is an over-3-hundred-year-old park named after the Pool of Drunken Bai, or Zuibai Chi. The park is built around the villa of Gu Dashen, a painter and official in the early Qing Dynasty who built the pool in honor of Li Bai (a famous poet in the Tang Dynasty who was drowned when he fell drunk into a pond, trying to grasp a reflection of the moon). Occupying an area of more than 90 *mus*, the park boasts its Inner Garden with a quadrate pool, extending corridors, meandering wave-topped walls,

Pool of Drunken Bai

elegant pavilions, terraces and buildings. East of the pool is a boathouse named Yifang. The corridor wall on the south of the pool is carved with 28 pictures and eulogies of the sages of Songjiang in the past dynasties.

Square Pagoda Park Occupying an area of about 200 *mus*, the Square Pagoda Park (Fangta Yuan) is named after the 48.5m square pagoda, which was built as part of the Xingshengjiao Temple. With wide eaves and bronze bells hanging on each corner, it looks graceful and unique among all the towers of China. On the west wall of the third floor there are two frescos dating back to the Song Dynasty. During the reconstruction in 1975 a brick vault containing a stone box with a gold-plated Buddha, silver cases, teeth relics of Buddha, ancient coins of the Tang and Song Dynasties and other relics were discovered under the foundations.

Square Pagoda Park

The screen wall in the north of the park shows a legendary monster with one buckhorn, glowering eyes, a lion tail, ox feet and dragon squamae. With vigorous but exquisite lines, this brick carving is a rare curiosa.

Jiading: An Enchanting Scenic Spot

Jiading is a river-surrounded small town located in the northwest of Shanghai. With a centuries-old history and brilliant culture, it has been one of Shanghai's satellitic towns of Science and Culture for a long time.

The Gate of Garden of Ancient Splendour

Garden of Ancient Splendour   Located in Nanxiang Town, the Garden of Ancient Splendour was built in the middle of the 16th century. The center of the garden is the Geese Pond. A richly ornamented boat perching in the east is called Buxi Boat, while the pavilion on the west, which is topped with a white crane, is named White Crane Pavilion and helps the town to win its reputation. Other beautiful scenes include the Bamboo Hill, the Fujun Pavilion and the Unfilled Corner Pavilion, which is a square pavilion but only with three unturned corners. This is to remind people of the national humiliation of the September 18 Accident when the three Northeastern Provinces of China, namely, Liaoning, Jilin and Heilongjiang, were occupied by Japanese invaders.

Garden of Autumn Clouds   Built in 1506, the Garden of Autumn Clouds (Qiuxia Pu) was the private garden of Gong Hong, a minister in the Ming Dynasty, and is one of the oldest gardens around Shanghai. It once had ten famous scenes including Pine Wind Hill, Orioles Singing Bank and Chill Fragrance Room, which were inscribed by Dong Qichang as "Shi Mu Zhi

Garden of Ancient Splendour

Jian" (within ten scenes). Just as the name tells, autumn is the best season to visit the Garden of Autumn Clouds.

Garden of Autumn Clouds

Confucius Temple   Built in 1219, the Confucius Temple (Kong Miao) is located on the South Street of Jiading and a shrine to pay devotion to Confucius, the most famous Chinese philosopher. With whitened walls, black tiles, flying eaves, coin like corners and brick and stone carvings, the temple looks simple, unsophisticated but, at the same time, majestic. The first thing greets you are three lofty memorial archways respectively named "Yang Shang", "Xing Xian" and "Yu Cai". Along the memorial archways you'll pass 72 carved lions squatting on the stone railings, representing the 72 outstanding disciples of Confucius. Most of the stone carvings date back to the Ming Dynasty. The main building at the Confucius Temple is the Dacheng Hall, which exhibits the statues of Confucius and his four most outstanding disciples. The backyard used to be the place of lecturing and now houses the scripts of many influential people.

Confucius Temple

← Xiyu Bridge in the Flowing Stream Garden

Qingpu: A Pearl of Watery Regions

A next-door neighbor of Jiangsu and Zhejiang Provinces, Qingpu is a typical watery town and has the largest fresh water lake around Shanghai, which

covers a water surface of 62 sq. km. and is 12 times as large as the West Lake in Hangzhou. A land flowing with milk and honey, it has gradually become a tourist attraction.

Flowing Stream Garden Built in 1745, the Flowing Stream Garden (Qushui Yuan) is one of the five classical gardens in Shanghai and named after the verse of Wang Xi: "drinking wine beside the flowing stream". With wide gates and courtyard, the 120-meter-long corridor as well as the camphor trees, cedar trees, flowers, bounding walls and lattice windows bringing out the best in each other, the garden provides a unique atmosphere. Isn't it a treat to sit in the garden and hear raindrops beating the palm leaves?

Flowing Stream Garden

Ancient Town Zhujiajiao   A typical watery town in Southern China, Zhujiajiao is of primitive simplicity with ponds and pools full of water caltrops and lotus, row upon row of ancient houses along the river, tropical vines coming down from grey tiles and eaves, small stores with signs flying in the wind dotted in the alleyways, women washing and talking around the well and boats with happily singing boatmen coming and going. The main sight in Zhujiajiao is the Captive-Animal Freeing Bridge (Fangsheng Qiao), which is 70.8 meters long, 5.8 meters wide and about 10 meters high and has five arches. Built in 1571, it looks like a rainbow spanning over the river and connecting two banks. From the instance it seems to be a hump sprouting out from the streets. The town has more than 20 stone bridges, which form another beautiful scene.

Jinze——Hometown of Bridges

Jinze: Hometown of Bridges   The ancient town Jinze is famous for its bridges and has the saying "getting down every bridge you see a temple and getting out every temple you see a bridge". The town occupies an area of only 0.5 sq. km. but had 42 bridges built in the Song and Yuan Dynasties. However, only 21 got preserved. The most famous bridges are Yingxiang Bridge, Wan'an Bridge and Puji Bridge. Built in 1335, Yingxiang Bridge is a 34.25-meter-long stone bridge with six supporting columns and five arches and looks like a beautiful rainbow spanning the river. The 29-meter-long Wan'an Bridge was built in 1260 and has only one arch and

Ancient Town Zhujiajiao

soft grading. Puji Bridge was built in 1267 and is 26.7 meters long. It's made of purple stones and shows the color whenever it rains. Other bridges include Tianwangge Bridge, Ruyi Bridge, Fangsheng Bridge, etc.

Grand View Garden

Grand View Garden   Located beside the Dianshan Lake, the Grand View Garden (Daguan Yuan) is a mock-up of the scenes and buildings from the famous Chinese classical novel *Dream of Red Mansions* (Hong Lou Meng). It is divided into two sections. The east section has thousands of plum trees and more than 4,000 cherry bays. A 380-meter-long causeway extending to the lake and fragrant flowers compete with each other for the battle of beauty. The west section occupies an area of 9 hectares and copies the descriptions and buildings in the novel.

Sun Island   Originally a sterile land, the national tourist resort Sun Island (Taiyang Dao) occupies an area of 2,350 *mus* and has a whole range of activities including a golf course, a 13,000 sq. m. international club, horse-riding, a shooting gallery, a tennis court and a gymnasium. With several hundred villas in various styles and a complete service of catering and entertainment, it's a best choice to relax yourself and have a fabulous holiday.

Sun Island

Oriental Boat   Previously the camping base for teenagers, the Oriental Boat (Dongfang Lvzhou), which is located on the west of the Dianshan Lake, keeps being an activity center of young people. It has bushy forests, small villas and camping tents and provides a complete service of catering, such as picnic and barbecue, and a whole range of activities including yachting, motorboating, skating, fishing, etc.

Nanhui: Key Door of the Sea

Situated in southeast Shanghai, Nanhui is a key door of the sea, neighboring Hangzhou Bay on the south, the East China Sea on the east and looking at each other with the Putuo Mountain (a famous Buddhist scenic spot), the Shengsi Island and the Zhoushan archipelago, the largest fishing port in China. Gradually Nanhui has developed itself into a golden littoral tourist line.

Luchao Harbor

Luchao Harbor: A Nature-born Good Harbor Located on the west bank of the Pacific Ocean and the bulgy middle part of the East China Sea and connected with the Yangtze River on the north, Luchao Harbor (Luchao Gang) of Nanhui commands the pass of all boats when they enter into the Yangtze River. With deep water and calm surface, it is reputed as the "Cape of Good Hope" on the western Pacific. A national open seaport, it now has lines to Singapore, Japan, Korea, Malaysia, Philippines, etc. and projects like the deep water port and the manpower byland are under construction.

Peach Blossom Festival Peach blossom has always been a symbol of goodliness and happiness in China and is thus liked by the Chinese people. Nanhui has held the Peach Blossom Festival (Taohua Jie) in succession for over ten years. At the festival, you can enjoy a sea of flowers of various colors, experience the countrified life like riding the waterwheel, working on the water mill, plowing by cow, weaving on the loom and fishing with net, and taste all delicacies of the countryside, including tuber onion cakes, muskmelon pies, shepherd's-purse wonton, fragrant bean curd and, of course, the juicy peaches. Besides, you will also be charmed by flying kites at the seaside, sipping tea and viewing the tides and working as a fishman.

Shanghai Wild Animals Park Located in Sanzhao Town of Nanhui, the Shanghai Wild Animals Park, the largest national wild animal park, occupies an area of 153 hectares and exhibits more than 200 kinds of rare animas totaling over 10,000. Guided by the tenet of "coexistence of humanity and nature", the park is divided into several sections according to the origins and habitats of different animals, making the trips both recreational and educational.

Peach Blossoms in Nanhui

Three Islands of Shanghai: Pearls in the Mouth of a Dragon

On the estuary of the Yangtze River there are three islands, namely, Chongming Island, Changxing Island and Hengsha Island. If we assimilate the Yangtze River to a giant dragon, these three islands are just like three bright pearls in the mouth of the dragon.

Chongming Island: Unrestrained and Far-ranging   The third island and also the No. 1 alluvion of China, Chongming Island occupies an area of 1,100 sq. km., about one sixth of Shanghai, and keeps expanding every year. It looks like a silkworm reclining on the estuary of the Yangtze River. The Chongming National Forest Park on the island occupies an area of 5,000 *mus* and provides a whole range of activities and services, including barbecue, picnic, horse-racing, rock-climbing, swimming, villas and hammocks. A pure land with no pollution, the east shoal of Chongming Island is listed as one of the national nature reserves and, every year, attracts numerous birds coming to live through the winter. It is the "Kidney of Green" in Shanghai.

Migrant Birds

Chongming Forest Park

Chongming Wetland Conservation Zone

Changxing Island: Heaven with Flowers and Fruits　Locally named "Ya Wo Sha", Changxing Island occupies an area of about 80 sq. km. and is a half-an-hour-drive from downtown. It appeared from the sea only about a hundred years ago and took shape 20 years ago. The island is also reputed as "the Island of Oranges" because there are stretches of orange orchards. With good weather and a favorable environment, it won the name of "Pure Island" and "Longevity Island".

Hengsha Island: Fairyland on Water　The first island on the estuary of the Yangtze River, Hengsha Island came out from the sea in 1864 and occupies an area of 40 sq. km. It is warm in winter and cool in summer and the temperature in summer is always 2-3℃ lower than that in downtown. With pure soil, pure water and pure air, it is one of Shanghai' s green food bases. Most of the people living here can lead a long life and the island is thus noted as China's "Island of Longevous People". East of the sea area is a fairyland co-built with Singapore, which boasts a whole range of activities on water, including motorboating, surfing, parachuting and yachting. You can also enjoy fresh seafood and have picnics or barbecues here.

Ripened Oranges on Changxing Island

Orange Orchards of Changxing Island

First Published in August 2005 by
SHANGHAI PEOPLE'S FINE ARTS PUBLISHING HOUSE
No.33, Lane 672, Changle Road
Shanghai, China (200040)

ACKNOWLEDGEMENTS:
Shanghai Municipal Tourism Administrative Commission
Party History Research Center of Huangpu District Party Committee of CPC
Shanghai Committee
Shanghai Xuhui District Tourism Bureau
Yuan Yinchang Design Studio

CHINESE TEXT: Shen Yicheng
TRANSLATOR: Fei Yuying
PHOTOGRAPHERS: Cai Xuzhou, Chen Kangling, Chen zhimin, Da Xiangqun, Ding
Jieren, Guo Changyao, Hang Zhizhong, Hong Li'en, Hou Jun, Jiang Jiaqi, Liu
Xiaotian, Pu Xingxing, Shao Liyang, Shen Yicheng, Shi Zhiqin, Tang Dewei, Tao
Hongxing, Wei Wen, Xiao Yi, Xu Hede, Xu Zhengkui, Xue Changming, Yang Li,
Yao Jianliang, Yuan Yinchang, Zhang Bingjue, Zhang Jiren, Zhang Wenrui, Zhao
Tianzuo, Zheng Xianzhang, Zou Yimin (in the alphabetical order of furnames)

CURATORS OF APPROACHING CHINA SERIES: Li Xin
EXECUTIVE EDITOR: Yu Ying, Zhang Cui
TECHNICAL EDITOR: Lu Yaochun
INTERIOR AND COVER DESIGN: Yuan Yinchang

Library of Congress Cataloging-in-Publication Data:
 Approaching China, Shanghai / Text by Shen Yicheng, Translated by Fei Yuying,
Photographed by Yuan Yinchang, etc. –Shanghai: Shanghai People's Fine Arts
Publishing House, 2005
 ISBN 7-5322-4508-X
 Ⅰ. Approaching... Ⅱ. Shen... Fei... Yuan... Ⅲ. Travell Guide--China--Picture Book,
Travell Guide--Shanghai City--Picture Book Ⅳ. K928.9-64
 Library of Chinese Cataloging-in-Publication Data (2005) No.087405

Printed in China by Shanghai zhong hua Printing Co.,Ltd.